Studies in
Writing & Rhetoric

IN 1980, THE CONFERENCE ON COLLEGE COMPOSITION AND COM-
munication perceived a need for providing publishing opportunities
for monographs that were too lengthy for publication in its journal
and too short for the typical publication of scholarly books by The
National Council of Teachers of English. A series called Studies in
Writing and Rhetoric was conceived, and a Publication Committee
established.

Monographs to be considered for publication may be speculative,
theoretical, historical, or analytical studies; research reports; or
other works contributing to a better understanding of writing, including interdisciplinary studies or studies in disciplines related to
composing. The SWR series will exclude textbooks, unrevised dis-
ertations, book-length manuscripts, course syllabi, lesson plans, and
collections of previously published material.

Any teacher-writer interested in submitting a work for publication in this series should send either a prospectus and sample manuscript or a full manuscript to the Senior Editor for Publications,
NCTE, 1111 Kenyon Road, Urbana, IL 61801. Accompanied by a
sample manuscript, a prospectus should contain a rationale, a definition of readership within the CCCC constituency, comparison
with related publications, an annotated table of contents an estimate
of length in double-spaced 8½ × 11 sheets, and the date by which
full manuscript can be expected. Manuscripts should be in range of
100 to 170 typed manuscript pages.

The works that have been published in this series serve as models
for future SWR monographs.

Something Old, Something New College Writing Teachers and Classroom Change

Wendy Bishop

WITH A FOREWORD BY PATRICK HARTWELL

Published for the Conference on College Composition and Communication

SOUTHERN ILLINOIS UNIVERSITY PRESS
Carbondale and Edwardsville

Production of works in this series has been partly funded by the
Conference on College Composition and Communication of the National
Council of Teachers of English.

Printed in the United States of America
Edited by Mara Lou Hawse
Designed by Design for Publishing, Inc., Bob Nance
Production supervised by Linda Jorgensen-Buhman

Library of Congress Cataloging-in-Publication Data

Bishop, Wendy.
    Something old, something new: college writing teachers and
classroom change / Wendy Bishop; with a foreword by Patrick
Hartwell.
        p.   cm.—(Studies in writing & rhetoric)
    "Published for the Conference on College Composition and
Communication."
    Includes bibliographical references (p.).
    1. English language—Rhetoric—Study and teaching.   I. Conference
on College Composition and Communication (U.S.).   II. Title.
III. Series.
PE1404.B57   1990
808'.042'07—dc20   89-27529
ISBN 0-8093-1601-3   CIP

93 92 91 90   4 3 2 1

The paper used in this publication meets the minimum requirements of
American National Standard for Information Sciences—Permanence of
Paper for Printed Library Materials, ANSI Z39.48-1984. ⊚

Contents

Foreword

Patrick Hartwell

MASTER TEACHER TOM BRIDGES IS, NECESSARILY, A FICTION, AS are the teachers who were his students in the graduate course, Teaching Basic Writing—Susan, Rosalyn, Peg, Nick, and Julia— taught at mythical Gatton University. And Wendy's story is, perforce, for the most part, "mere narrative." But this narrative rings true, as we say of good fiction, and Wendy's observations have the texture of felt life.

There is much to be said about Tom Bridges. He knows his field, and he teaches a course that is neither lockstep nor idiosyncratic. His focus is current, reputable, and national. He does not trivialize the discipline, and he obviously respects his learners. The students explore techniques to use in class, like sentence combining, but Tom Bridges rightly chooses to emphasize higher order concerns, the theories of language and of learning that undergird how we behave as teachers.

Students do not always (or ever) learn what we teach—that's evident in what teachers internalize from Tom Bridges's classroom, and it's equally evident in their own classrooms. But they face horrendous teaching loads and often uncongenial environments. The moral here, despite—or even because of—the diversity of responses, is a positive one. These are independent, self-motivated learners, and Tom Bridges wisely decides to let research findings speak for themselves.

Wendy's stories are rich in metaphors; again, necessarily so. Texts play off against texts, and conversations build on conversations. The dominant metaphor, for make-believe Tom, real Wendy, make-believe Susan, Rosalyn, Peg, Nick, and Julia (and real Pat Hartwell, at least one of them), is a religious one, conversion. Despite the reasoned nature of the course, the final decision these teachers must make is a personal one—how willing am I to trust language?

I see this course with a somewhat different metaphor, helped by my daughter Beth, the dancer. When I see Beth dance, I watch the moves that I saw in the dancing of her mentor and teacher. I see Tom Bridges as a mentor, as well as a teacher, and I see his students, in some sense, dancing.

This monograph deserves a wider audience than the obvious one of graduate level teacher-educators, for I can't think of a better introduction to modern approaches to composition, dramatizations of what good teachers do in good classrooms. It ought to be made available to graduate teaching assistants entering the profession, and it would serve as the best available resource to those within the profession who are curious about new theories of teaching composition.

Though it's just a story, or rather a series of stories, I take storytelling seriously, for, in some sense, we write out our lives as narrative texts. These teacher/students take many risks, professional and personal. We owe them thanks for allowing us to observe their learning, and we owe many thanks to Tom Bridges, although, unlike others, I would not like to grow up to be like him.

Acknowledgments

First thanks go to the case study teachers, Julia, Nick, Peg, Rosalyn, and Susan, who cheerfully collected materials and willingly opened their classrooms to observation. These individuals became friends and respected colleagues. Additionally, the teachers enrolled in the Teaching Basic Writing pedagogy seminar donated hours of their time, and each contributed to the description of that classroom and graduate program culture.

Tom Bridges, the seminar instructor, also gave hours of his own and his classroom time. Not only did he agree to permit a participant-observer into his classroom but he also reviewed my observations and entered fully into the ethnographic process, correcting my vision and detailing his world view in a way that illuminated and enlarged my understanding.

During the course of the study, Pat Hartwell and Mike Williamson offered needed and always useful advice. Don McAndrew provided invaluable help by reviewing the research design, discussing ongoing research concerns, and, finally, making careful readings of a number of drafts. A model scholar, researcher, and teacher, he challenged me to work to the best of my abilities, and I thank him for his support and friendship. Flaws in this study are entirely my responsibility, but credit for forbearance and encouragement goes to those individuals I have mentioned and to some I may have neglected to mention.

Thanks to Michael Spooner and members of the review committee for the Studies in Writing and Rhetoric series for supporting research on writing teachers, to Kenney Withers and Susan Wilson of Southern Illinois University Press, and to Mara Lou Hawse for editing.

Finally, I am grateful that Marvin Pollard and Morgan Pollard Bishop and Tait Bishop Pollard survived this experience with unfailing good nature.

Introduction

The ethnographer in local scenes must . . . make the familiar strange to come to an understanding of it. (Mehan, 1982, p. 61)

THIS BOOK EXPLORES THE COMPLEX WORLD OF THE COLLEGE writing teacher at work. Such a teacher develops classroom knowledge as she moves from a beginning to an experienced teacher. And sometimes after years in the classroom, she may decide to become a reentry graduate student. I was interested in this college level teacher of writing who returns to doctoral program work in composition to learn more about her field, for I had been such a returning writing teacher myself—one who found the experience powerful *and* problematic. I wanted to describe what learning was valuable and how such a teacher of writing used her degree work to inform her subsequent college writing classroom.

Like all projects, this one was grounded in a wealth of questions which included, but were not limited to, the following:

1. After college writing teachers have undergone a teacher training course, what significant affective, cognitive, or pedagogical changes will they have undergone?
2. Are the changes short-term or long-term?
3. How do teachers develop a theoretical base for teaching and how well do they reflect such a base in their classroom teaching practices? Is

such a base present when they begin a doctoral program and/or enter a pedagogy seminar, or does it develop as a result of the doctoral program and the pedagogy seminar?

4. What influence do any preexisting attitudes toward or beliefs about composition have on teachers' abilities to change through the course of a pedagogy seminar and after their return to the writing classroom?

A preliminary bibliographic review confirmed that much work remains to be done in this area. Few research studies of teachers as learners are available, particularly at the college level, although a great number of teacher training programs, teacher preservice and in-service workshops, and writing across the curriculum workshops are reported (Boirsky, 1980; Brannon & Pradl, 1984; Burnham, 1984; Garnes, 1984; Moran, 1981; Roberts, 1982), most modeled on the Bay Area Writing Project (BAWP) and the National Writing Project (NWP).

The available research relies primarily on teacher self-report, usually collected through post-training questionnaires (Poulin & White, 1985; Thomas, 1979; Thompson, 1979). Self-report studies often consist of tabulated questionnaires, post-training interviews, and relatively little follow-up of teachers when they return to their teaching classrooms. Exceptions include Perl and Wilson's (1986) longitudinal ethnographic study of elementary and secondary teachers. Daniels and Zemelman (1985) report that, in post-testing, students of Illinois writing project teachers exhibited twice the improvement as that of students of non-project teachers, and their study includes teachers' self-descriptions of positive affective and pedagogical change. However, the work of Perl and Wilson (1986) and Daniels and Zemelman (1985) focused on writing teachers at the pre-college level.

To understand the goals and structure of a *graduate level* training course for teachers of writing and to describe teacher change and development through participation in such a course and after teachers return to their classrooms, it is worth reviewing the dominant models of college writing teacher training that are currently in place in U.S. institutions.

College level teacher training has most often been concerned with the preparation (or lack of preparation) of English department graduate teaching assistants (GTAs) who make up from one-half to two-thirds of the teaching staff in most English departments today (Berlin, 1987; Neel, 1978; Young, 1986). Traditionally, these novice writing teachers are assigned classes and given textbooks; then, with no further preparation, they are asked to instruct freshman writers. Recent scholars claim this is changing (Corbett, 1987; Purdy, 1986) because of training programs developed by English departments and the rise of doctoral programs in rhetoric and linguistics that are producing a cadre of more fully trained writing program administrators and teachers (see Chapman & Tate, 1987, for a review of doctoral programs).

Training programs for teaching assistants follow the same general outline, with a few variations. Graduate teaching assistants participate in a pre-semester teaching orientation meeting or a workshop of three to five days, modeled on the Bay Area Writing Project and the National Writing Project where teachers are encouraged to write and to learn small-group critiquing methods. They are also asked to work in groups, to evaluate sample student papers, and to prepare a first semester curriculum guide if a standardized guide is not prepared by the department (Brannon & Pradl, 1984; Donovan 1984; Gracie, 1982; Moran, 1981; Newkirk, 1983).

While teaching their first writing courses, many GTAs enroll concurrently in their department's graduate seminar for training writing teachers. Elements of such a seminar may include a review of theories in the field of composition studies, the historical study of rhetoric, student presentation of successful teaching practices, student-kept class logs, and teacher-trainer and/or department mentor's visitation to the GTA's writing classroom.

Variations on this model are largely dependent on department funding, but beyond funding concerns, GTA preparation may be influenced by program commitment to composition studies. That is, those departments that offer graduate degrees with a composition or rhetoric option may have more pedagogy courses available for teaching assistants or program participants (Smith, 1984).

Courses in the teaching of writing at the university level, for graduate programs in rhetoric or composition, appear to place a strong emphasis on understanding and conducting research, theory building, *and* composition pedagogy. Chapman and Tate (1987) found that a pedagogy class in composition was the single common element across fifty-three institutions reporting doctoral programs with rhetoric components. These courses may be taught as surveys of current research and theory, as historical surveys of composition studies and rhetoric (what I term a *competing theories* model of instruction), or as more unitary, new paradigm, process theory-based seminars, such as the one I studied (what I term a *convergent theory* model of instruction).

College-level teacher trainers are concerned with defining the constituent elements of a writing pedagogy course. The efficacy and appropriateness of the BAWP/NWP-derived survey of theories model, advocated by trainers like Haring-Smith (1985) who believes teachers benefit from the study of competing theories, is being challenged by some teacher trainers like Ruszkiewicz (1987) who claims, "I found myself less satisfied with what I was actually doing— offering novice instructors a smorgasbord of theories, techniques, terms, and names every respectable writing teacher should know. I began to sense that it was possible to be a respectable writing teacher without being a good one" (p. 461).

Ruszkiewicz argues that teacher trainers should model the process of teaching more thoroughly, something the survey-based model may not allow them to do. Brooke contributes to the complexity of this issue by claiming that the business of writing classrooms and writing teachers is the development of students' identities. In "Modeling a Writer's Identity," Brooke (1988) explains, "The entire 'process, not product' revolution can be seen as a change of focus from results to behaviors, from texts to people—in its best forms, the goal is to teach people to be writers, not to produce good texts in the course of a semester" (pp. 38–39). In another article concerned with similar issues, "'Underlife' and Writing Instruction," Brooke (1987) describes the consequences of this shift in pedagogical focus. "Writing instruction is thus a *disruptive* form of underlife, a form which tries to undermine the nature of the institution and posit a different one in its place" (p. 151). The teacher of a convergent theory writing pedagogy classroom, therefore, might be working unabashedly to change teachers' behaviors and teachers' identities, and might also be working to change teachers' institutions by so changing the teachers.

Currently, the prevalent model for college teacher training appears to be the competing theories model. However, a few teacher trainers and pedagogy theorists like Ruszkiewicz, Brooke, and others are beginning to discuss and question the efficacy of such a system and to advocate an ideologically explicit, convergent theory model of college-level writing teacher training. Such thinking is supported by Shor (1987) (as an interpreter of Paulo Freire), Newkirk (1983), and Giroux (1981) who insist that no teacher training program or pedagogy seminar can actually be ideologically neutral. For, as Giroux explains, "Methods of curriculum design, implementation, and evaluation must be seen as a construction in values and ideology" (p. 159).

Added to these social, theoretical, and methodological concerns will be the reality of college level writing teacher diversity: teachers in any program may range from pure novice (twenty-two-year-old students beginning an M.A. degree program in English) to experienced, although not necessarily proficient, teacher (re)trainees (fifty-year-old teachers with twenty years of classroom teaching experience who are working on a doctorate in rhetoric, as were several of the teachers found in my study). Teacher trainers may expect wide variations in the same pedagogy seminar in teacher preparation, expectations, and attitudes.

The Research Model

This review of research into writing teacher training underscored the complexity of the phenomena I was intending to study: the world of the writing teacher is highly interactive. It includes many "players" and cannot be fruitfully understood out of context. To study teachers as they moved from their pedagogy seminar to their own classrooms, I turned to ethnographic modes of inquiry that allowed me to use both qualitative and quantitative data-gathering techniques (Wilcox, 1982). The hallmark of such work in educational anthropology is a researcher's interest in studying the learning or educational process in a cultural context (Kamil, Langer, & Shanahan, 1985).

Since the late 1960s, there has been increased interest in this methodology in educational research. Interest and practice began to encompass "studies that were termed qualitative, field-oriented, observational, cross-cultural, or ethnographic" (Goetz & LeCompte, 1984, p. 27). Ethnographic studies involve a major paradigmatic shift from a prevailing experimental tradition. The ethnographic mode, based in a cultural context, presents a phenomenological and empirical approach to research. It is holistic and naturalistic (Goetz & LeCompte, 1984; Kamil, Langer, & Shanahan, 1985).

Currently, distinctions are being drawn between macro- and microethnographies. Macroethnographies report research on multiple sites and involve larger or longer projects than do microethnographies. Microethnographies, like this study, can report on the culture of the single classroom, the single learner, and even the single learning event (Goetz & LeCompte, 1984; Kamil, Langer, & Shanahan, 1985; Spradley, 1980; Wolcott, 1982).

Ethnographic inquiry can be misapplied or misconceived. Too often, research using a single ethnographic technique (case study, life history interviewing, participant observation, and so on) is claimed as full-scale ethnography, resulting in what Rist (1980) calls "blitzkreig ethnography." Poorly designed studies may do what North (1987) fears—contribute to a research "community with borders but no center" (p. 313). To avoid misapplication, ethnographic data analysis must derive its reliability and validity from a fully developed scheme of data collection, data reduction, data display, and conclusion drawing/verification which takes place recursively, with steps being repeated and refined until conclusions may safely be presented (Miles & Huberman 1984). Additionally, data is collected by more than one method (interviews, direct observation, artifacts) in order to assure triangulation, verification from multiple sources, while research reports rely on the "thick description" described and utilized by Geertz (1973, 1983).

Ethnographic methodology can supply important cultural and contextual data that has not been provided by more limited survey studies relating to teacher training mentioned above. Additionally, the ethnographic methodology reflects recent trends in the field of composition and rhetoric research to develop "a model of inquiry appropriate to our own discipline—composition as a part of English studies—consistent with its values, supporting and enlightening it" (Irmscher, 1987, p. 82).

Given these considerations, I chose an ethnographic methodology and narrative as my means of reporting research data from my desire to *describe* writing teachers' lives rather than from an intention to develop or *prove* a theory of teaching. Brodkey (1987b) discusses many issues of concern in ethnographic reporting, including whether such information should be presented as "analysis" from a cognitive research perspective or as "interpretation" from a social research perspective. Although built on careful analysis, my narratives grow out of the social research perspective. And in offering these case studies, I do not deny the problem of my own presence in and interpretation of these teachers' teaching lives (see also Van Maanen, 1988, for a taxonomy of narrative styles).

Nonetheless, I agree with Brodkey that incessant methodological arguments may be keeping us from discovering what really can be learned from an ethnographic study. She describes a problem of qualitative versus quantitative research paradigms in general when she explains, "And of course, as we persist in finding one another unspeakably rational or empirical and everyone else unbearably 'subjective' we are likely to spend our lives talking to ourselves" (1987b, p. 42). Or as Laing (1969) explained as he worked to describe a "science of persons," "It is interesting, for example, that one frequently encounters 'merely' before subjective, whereas it is almost inconceivable to speak of anyone being 'merely' objective" (p. 25). Rather than rearguing the methodology problem here, I move on to emphasizing, with Brodkey, that "Ethnography attempts to bring stories not yet heard to the attention of the academy" (p. 48). While these teachers' stories might prompt further research or might result in future theories of instruction, most immediately they will be worth listening to if they tell us about our own teaching and our own writing classrooms.

The Study

During 1987–1988, I completed qualitative data collection which allowed me to describe the progress of a class of teachers of college writing who were newly enrolled in a Ph.D. program in English/ Rhetoric and Linguistics at Gatton University,[1] a medium-size university in the northeast. These teachers enrolled in an intensive

1. The names of teachers, professors, and the institution in this research study have been changed, but data have been shared with these individuals and appear with their consent.

summer program and took one of the doctoral program's core courses entitled "Teaching Basic Writing," a pedagogy course designed by the rhetoric program to study "characteristics of the writing process and of the basic writer, methods for the evaluation of writing and approaches to the teaching of writing." As a participant-observer in the pedagogy seminar during the summer of 1987, I was able to observe thirteen enrolled writing teachers in the flux of pedagogical development and change.

I conducted case studies of five of these teachers as they returned to their college classrooms, fall 1987, with the intention of implementing new teaching practices, based on what the teacher trainer, Dr. Thomas A. Bridges, described as "the whole language, writing workshop" classroom model. This model emphasized student-generated writing assignments, student peer groups, classroom conferencing, portfolio evaluation, and so on.

Of the five teachers, two taught at community colleges and three taught at four-year colleges; two taught pre-freshman level classes of college writing and three taught freshman level classes; four were female and one was male (two other male teachers began but did not complete the case study data collection). The teachers' home institutions were geographically diverse, located in Florida, Oregon, Pennsylvania, South Carolina, and Virginia.

Data sources for the Teaching Basic Writing seminar included surveys, interviews with all thirteen seminar members, participant-observer field notes, and teachers' extensive seminar learning logs and final class projects (see the Appendix for an overview of data collection and analysis). For the case study teachers' fall writing classrooms, data sources included phone interviews, teachers' journals, classroom surveys, classroom documents (student papers and teachers' handouts), and classroom videotapes. By analyzing and triangulating data from multiple sources and reconfirming data with the teachers themselves during follow-up interviews in 1987 and 1988, I was able to describe the ways in which these teachers changed or resisted classroom change. In forming my narratives I had for models the voices in Glenda Bissex's *GNYS AT WRK: A Child Learns to Write and Read* (1980); Lucy McCormick Calkins' *Lessons from a Child* (1983); Jerome Harste, Virginia Woodward, and Carolyn Burke's *Language Stories and Literacy Lessons* (1984); Shirley Brice Heath's *Ways with Words* (1983); Sondra Perl and

Nancy Wilson's *Through Teachers' Eyes* (1986), and others. For my descriptions I do not claim the authority of those long-term, longitudinal studies where researchers lived with or studied writers, teachers, families, and, sometimes, communities for years at a time. Nevertheless, my interaction with these teachers was intense as I enrolled in their pedagogy seminar, interviewed them, and shared learning with them during the summer of 1987. I had added insight into their community of knowledge due to my previous enrollment in the Teaching Basic Writing seminar during the summer of 1985. At that time, two years before this study was undertaken, I was a doctoral student at the same university, learning about composition pedagogy from the same professor, and I returned in the fall of 1985 to my writing classroom at my home university to put theory into practice. It was an invigorating, frustrating, exciting semester and one which eventually led to the questions raised in this research project.

Beginning my research two years later, I was careful to "make the familiar strange" (Mehan, 1982, p. 61). I could not assume that these teachers' experiences would at all reflect my own. However, my position as a "senior discourse student" in the rhetoric program and my sympathy towards and essential understanding of their activities gave me immediate access to the teachers' ever-changing and developing community during the summer of 1987 and to the varied communities of their home institutions as I kept in close contact with the five case study teachers throughout the fall of 1987. By presenting five case studies in which I compare and discuss similar data *across cases* I hope to present the fullest possible picture and a useful portrait of college writing teachers and classroom change (Yin, 1984).

Chapter 1 describes a class of thirteen teachers as learners in the Gatton University doctoral program in English/rhetoric and during the pedagogy seminar, Teaching Basic Writing. Chapters 2 through 6 present five case study teacher narratives. In each case study, I relate material in parallel order, although individual themes surface for each teacher. I introduce a teacher, review her writing and teaching background, describe her reactions to the doctoral program and training seminar, and detail her teaching concerns. Next, the teacher's fall 1987 writing classroom is described briefly, and each case study ends with a discussion that summarizes and analyzes issues raised in the narrative. In order to discuss the change and development of these teachers, I review, in chapter 7, the study findings across cases and introduce relevant work of theorists in composition, psychology, and sociology as possible filters for viewing the complex worlds of college writing teachers and writing classrooms.

Something Old, Something New

Training Teachers in a Graduate Program in Rhetoric

Researcher: You're responding pleasurably to the program. Can you give me specifics?

Doctoral Student: Well, as a person, first of all, I know that I'm going to earn a Ph.D. I mean when I got, before I came here, I didn't know if I would be able to do it or not. Uh, I have been pushed and pushed and pushed. I'm going to score a 4.0 and it's going to be great. And I'm going to feel great about myself as a result. I'm going to make a raise when I go back. But, I think most of what I'm getting out of this is being a professional. As a teacher, I think, I think I'm going to be a very very different teacher than what I was before.

—Interview transcript, summer 1987

DOCTORAL STUDENTS AT GATTON UNIVERSITY ENROLL IN ONE OF two options for study offered by the English/Rhetoric and Linguistics program. The traditional option requires on-campus, academic year residency. Students take the required core curriculum and electives, pass comprehensive exams in three areas, and complete a research dissertation. The nontraditional option allows currently employed teachers (or writing program administrators) to enroll for courses during a minimum of two consecutive summers. Teachers also complete academic year independent study projects. The rest of their program includes the exams and dissertation mentioned above. Approximately two-thirds of the participants in this study were those in the nontraditional strand of the doctoral program: that is, they were currently employed teachers of writing who enrolled in the the doctoral program and its pedagogy seminar during summer session 1987.

At the time of this study, the *average* rhetoric doctoral program student at Gatton was a female college teacher, thirty-one to forty years of age, who had ten years of teaching experience, belonged to more than one professional organization like the Conference on College Composition and Communication (CCCC), National Council of Teachers of English (NCTE), etc., and subscribed to more than two professional journals. And this average student did some memo or business writing, kept a journal sporadically, and wrote personal letters and an occasional essay or article or piece of creative writing.

As they began doctoral study, most teachers expressed some sense of dissonance with their current teaching practices and said they hoped or expected to change due to their enrollment in the program. Although most teachers evaluated themselves as good or adequate writers and were looking forward to being doctoral students, many teachers nevertheless felt isolated from the mainstream of composition studies, subscribing to—but often not reading—journals, rarely attending national conventions, and, in general, appearing disconnected to the field of rhetoric and composition due to heavy teaching loads that left little time for professional development.

Here is one teacher describing his situation before he enrolled in rhetoric graduate studies.

> *Teacher:* I had a sense that I was so busy with work that I was missing out on all the research and scholarship being done in the field.
> *Researcher:* How did you know there was research and scholarship being done in the field?
> *Teacher:* Well, every once in a while I'd have enough time to look at a journal—so I really wanted to—renew, I wanted to go back to school to renew my enthusiasm and to learn about things that I knew I was falling behind on. So that was—profesional development, whatever you want to call it.

Seeking professional development was difficult because of a lack of time or because of teaching pressures, but sometimes it was because of a teacher's sense of being an outsider to an insider's system, as described by this teacher.

Teacher: I would glance occasionally at *CCC* just almost as a way of responding to a, just as a knee-jerk reaction, like, "Well I better do this." So I'd pick it up—I don't know what tagmemics means. You know I don't know what semiotics means. Ah, I had this attitude, "Oh, so they're not really concerned about me, the working teacher, they're talking all this theory, inventing words and using a jargon that really doesn't help me every Monday, Wednesday, Friday in the classroom." So I had a tendency to see the journals as highbrow stuff. Almost as a way of [the journal's] saying, "Well, we're sorry. If you have to read anything, try reading *Teaching English in the Two-Year College.*" Okay. So I had developed this kind of cynicism as a way of disguising my inadequacy. That it wasn't that I don't know what's going on—it was, "They [journals] don't know what I'm all about. So why should I try to learn?"

Additionally, many teachers were worried about their ability to leave their homes for summer study and succeed in a demanding doctoral program environment. This student honestly described her anxiety by explaining how she tried to "prepare" for her planned graduate work.

Teacher: I tried to do some reading to get ready for this [doctoral program]. Now, it wasn't reading. You know, I called to see if I could get a syllabus or a reading list. Nobody had a reading list for me. So, I just decided to do some reading, any kind of reading. You know, I mean I read, uh, fiction and I got really worried, Wendy, because I would read. I would try. I would set a goal for myself that I was going to try to read two books a week, you know, and some of them were little. Some of them were 150 pages and some of them were 400. Some of them were John Updike and some of them were, you know, maybe, I read some Hemingway.
Researcher: Would it be fair to say at that point, I'm thinking just because of the books you chose, that you didn't have a real clear concept of what you would be reading once you got here?
Teacher: No, I had no idea. The only thing I knew———

Researcher: You didn't know Thomas Kuhn from Flower and Hayes at that point?

Teacher: The only thing I knew. I had no idea who they were. Never. Uh. Now, what, and probably had I got that stuff it would have scared me away.

[*later in the same interview*]

Researcher: You were starting to say something, I think, about you maybe couldn't get those two books a week read?

Teacher: Oh yes. I couldn't. I couldn't. Because I would sit up at night to try to read—and this is after I've been grading papers since six o'clock at night—sit up and try to read and fall asleep. So I would go downstairs to the kitchen table and try to read.

Researcher: So you increased your anxiety about the program because you weren't sure that once you got here you could do that?

Teacher: Yes.

Often, those who did enroll came for a mixed set of reasons, from a desire to achieve personal validation by attaining a higher degree, to job-related reasons, such as being required by their departments to obtain a Ph.D. This teacher explains his reasons for enrolling.

Researcher: Why did you want it [a Ph.D]?

Teacher: I wanted it. That's a good question. I think there were two reasons and the two reasons remain. The primary reason is for personal fulfillment. I mean I'm a high school teacher and I really don't know if I'm ever going to do anything else because I like what I'm doing; it pays fairly well, and uh, even though I may wish to move from the school district that I'm in at the moment to a different one, I don't know that the professional, that I have a real professional goal. It's a personal goal; it's a personal fulfillment. Uh, I'd be the first person, I'm the first person with a master's degree, one of the first college graduates in my whole extended family. And I'd certainly be the first one with a Ph.D. Although it's a personal, it's an ego thing; there's no question about it. On the other hand, I've been a part-time college teacher for seven or eight years at [college name] in [town, state]. It's a four-year liberal arts college. Uh, and I really like college teaching. And I am going to try, probably next year before I complete my degree, I'm going to try for employment at the college level. So, my reason for going on for the Ph.D. is professionally motivated too. But that's really a secondary goal. It's really personal as the primary reason.

These teachers all viewed themselves as more process paradigm oriented than their colleagues at their home institutions, and they were viewed by Gatton University doctoral program professors as being fairly homogenous in background and slightly more prepared pedagogically than previous entering classes. However, although on survey forms they indicated fairly wide acquaintance with scholars and researchers in the field of composition studies, these teachers had not read many, if any, of the listed works in much depth, pointing to a superficial acquaintance with composition theory and research and possibly even with process pedagogy.

Life in the Doctoral Program

Participating in the doctoral program immediately immersed teachers in an environment that was both familiar and strange. After leaving home to enroll in summer classes, some teachers found such immersion overwhelming at first, placing stress on their personal or familial relationships and making them wonder if they could endure their course of study. Other teachers found that the immersion and isolation offered much-needed and desired focused study time in a field of great interest to them.

Peer networks developed in the University dormitories and through coursework; teachers met informally before or after seminars or in work groups to complete class-mandated projects. Program lore existed and was transmitted by word of mouth and in a few department documents. Returning teachers mentored new program participants and tried to calm their fears. For instance, all new doctoral program participants were alarmed at the sheer amount of reading and writing they were expected to do. Returning teachers would tell them to prioritize, to skip or skim reading materials; they would offer computer help and reading time (editing and critiquing seminar papers) to help new teachers cope. Those teachers who chose not to network, because they were commuting, were shy, or felt like "outsiders," sometimes had a less positive program outlook during interviews.

Program courses were unexpectedly rigorous for some teachers who came from a literature studies tradition or who had an under-developed understanding of the demands of doctoral level course-work. Those who completed their first few classes successfully, how-ever, usually found such success exhilarating and even talked about looking forward to returning the next summer as "senior discourse students" and to mentoring new program participants.

Finally, teachers in the doctoral program had to sort out program demands from individual course demands. As new doctoral program participants they were being initiated into a particular program ide-ology, and they were being asked to review, organize, and evaluate vast amounts of literature in the field of composition studies *and* to become writers of such material by producing publishable-quality seminar papers. The doctoral participant viewpoint often required teachers to be highly critical, to doubt, evaluate, balance, and sort through sometimes conflicting theories and sometimes poorly writ-ten or ill-conceived research reports (as well as a goodly amount of well-written material).

In different doctoral program seminars, teachers might also be asked to accede to a particular classroom ideology, such as that pre-sented in the Teaching Basic Writing seminar studied here. Teach-ers had to activate their professional teacher identity simultaneously with their new and developing doctoral program participant identity (and sometimes had friendships and informal social interactions with professors and peers outside of seminars which required a further negotiation of identity). Identity sorting, both personal and private, and identity shifting were major considerations for those enrolled in this program and this seminar. Here is one teacher describing his feelings.

Teacher: The intensity of the program, at the same time all of us are aware that all of us have things going on inside us that aren't course-related at the time, and when those things come into conflict, there's probably going to be a certain kind of mental paralysis.

Researcher: And you're talking about life, life history problems or strains, things that are going on in your own life beyond the program? Private life or—

Teacher: No, I'm talking about those kinds of things, the materials showed you the way you used to teach, that the coming into conflict with

the material itself, okay, and the pressures that, that———
Researcher: Who you were as a teacher and who you want to be?
Teacher: No, the personal life. Hey. Who has a personal life?
Researcher: It's another layer?
Teacher: It's something—it's completely—and that's one of the things I mentioned to [teacher's name] about her letter. I said, or about her little guide [for new, incoming doctoral students]. I said how about putting something in here about how to deal with loved ones and how to ask them for their patience because this is, my personal life is somewhere else right now.
Researcher: Yeah. I think most people find that it's very stressful.
Teacher: My gosh!

Stress of this sort alone caused a few doctoral program participants to remain only a day or two and then return to their homes. At the same time, some teachers valued this chance to sort things out.

Teacher: That's that's another wonderful thing this program has. Uh, to do this kind of thing, one needs total immersion and that's what this program, the summer program, gives you.
Researcher: Why do you need immersion? I'm interested in that phrase— "to do this thing?" So clearly you're seeing that something is happening to people as they're immersed here?
Teacher: Um. That's part of maybe speeding up the process of putting all the pieces together. Whereas if you're still leading a real life and trying to tend, do it [laughter], obviously your energy is dissipated and your focus is dissipated. And you know, I can't help think of my good friend who's supposedly taking comps at [the University of California at] Irvine and she's got three beautiful teenage kids and a job and you know, talking to me over the phone, saying, "Susan, can I come up to Oregon and study in your trailer?" You know [laughs]. And she just can't get away. She can't do what she needs in terms of getting away. Now, her family's very supportive. It doesn't mean her family's not supportive, but she needs to get away from them, right? Period.
Researcher: So in a certain sense, for all of you, this is a luxurious time as well as—stressful?
Teacher: Oh. It's a stressful time, but it's a luxury. In some ways it's very much, but it's a necessary luxury. I think. I'm really seeing it as a necessity, too. And it's not just a function of the time frame. Uh, oh, it's an

intensive program and we have to totally immerse ourselves because I think I'm gaining much more because of the total immersion, with or without the time constraints.

Clearly, enrollment in the doctoral program drew heavily on a teacher's resources for seeing herself in multiple contexts and for being able to tolerate ambiguity, hypocrisy, and/or paradoxical (mis)matching of roles. It also introduced challenging cognitive demands.

Pedagogy Seminar Structure

Tom Bridges divided Teaching Basic Writing, the pedagogy seminar, into three nearly equal sections. He designed the course to introduce participants to research into composing and teaching during the first (theory) section. He hoped this research would prepare teachers intellectually to accede to the idea of a whole language classroom. He defined such a classroom during interviews.

Bridges: I'd be very happy if that someone [teacher] when I looked in their classroom was creating something that would be what I'm now calling the whole language classroom—the classroom that is formed by that kind of workshop atmosphere, with everybody writing and responding and so on.

Researcher: What were you calling it [the pedagogical model] before?

Bridges: Uh, I think I was calling it writing-process, student-centered; student-centered, writing-process classroom was the phrase I was actually using. But I found it—Applebee, are we reading Applebee for today?

Researcher: Tomorrow

Bridges: Tomorrow. Okay. I think he's right. We've made that the center and we've made it in too simplistic a way. So I'm dropping back to another term that's more popular in elementary classrooms, and that is the whole language classroom, to suggest the, the interactive nature of the kind of beast that we're trying to create in our work life.

During the second (pedagogy) section of the course, the seminar focused on creating a model of the ideal whole language classroom through the analysis of teaching techniques that would achieve that end: in-class conferencing, the writers' workshop and collaborative classroom, portfolio grading, etc. The final (issues) section of the course consisted of miscellaneous but important topics in teaching writing (from writing across the curriculum [WAC] to computer assisted instruction [CAI]).

After acceding to the whole language classroom model through readings, demonstrations, and discussion, participants were asked to commit themselves to the use of this model in a written document, a sample curriculum guide *and rationale,* which showed how they would implement such a classroom. Participants *could* choose other final projects—a research proposal or grant proposal or a publishable paper—but most, in this seminar as well as in previous years' seminars, chose the curriculum guide and rationale, and class discussions often focused on designing such a guide.

Readings for the Teaching Basic Writing (TBW) seminar were current, especially the photocopied research articles, a packet that ran to 430 pages. In addition to producing a final seminar paper, Bridges asked teachers to keep a learning log and to meet in groups of three or four, for one hour, twice a week, to read and comment on each others' logs.

The tripartite organization of the seminar—(1) theory and research, (2) pedagogical applications of theory and research, and (3) important issues in composition—was clearly planned and announced in class. (Bridges would say, "Okay, today's an important day. During the second hour we switch from theory to practice.") But also, individual readings were so ordered as to form a dialog or an ongoing argument to support the whole language classroom model. Therefore, in the theory section of TBW, participants first read an introduction to the field, "Composing Processes: An Overview," by Bizzell (1986). Next, they read through primary process theory and research in "A Cognitive Process Theory of Writing," by Flower and Hayes (1981). Then, they read an extension of that work, "Composing Written Sentences," by Kaufer, Hayes, and Flower (1986).

While reading Perl's 1979 study, "The Composing Process of Unskilled College Writers," participants developed views of skilled and unskilled writers which prepared them for the next two readings: Flower's (1979) "Writer-Based Prose," which offered a possible explanation of why unskilled writers write as they do, and Rose's (1980) "Rigid Rules, Inflexible Plans, and the Stifling of Language," which furthered this discussion.

The entire research and theory section ended with another overview, "Problems in Process Approaches" by Applebee (1986), which portrays the fate of process pedagogies much less optimistically. Teachers had read through study after study showing how students compose, and they felt they must enhance a student's composing process in their own classrooms. The Applebee article—which argues that process models have fared poorly in American classrooms—was used by Bridges to signal the seminar's movement to pedagogical discussions. Reading it made the teachers close ranks, for under Bridges's guidance, they agreed that they *could, must,* and *would* solve the implementation problems that Applebee examines.

Thereafter, the class discussed teaching strategies, but the instructor continually guided participants toward developing and articulating an ideal, model classroom. They were not allowed the atomistic lists and sheets of teaching techniques they had thought they wanted. Rather, they were encouraged to develop a holistic model of teaching. Tom Bridges sometimes asked for patience and spoke of "pieces coming together" in order to encourage participants not to come to closure too soon. Reviewing the seminar syllabus for future readings, participants knew they couldn't and shouldn't come to closure while important issues were on future class agendas: teaching grammar, structuring assignments, evaluating writing, and so on. The seminar structure, therefore, did not allow participants to complete the curriculum guide, even should they wish to, until the last week.

The curriculum guide itself was a formulaic instrument, designed to show participants' understanding and acceptance of the model writing classroom. Sample curriculum guides were on reserve in the library. Teachers who read these sample papers noted in their seminar learning logs that the guides all seemed the same, listing similar classroom modes, activities, and evaluation procedures, and citing the same seminar-generated list of research in composition. This was not surprising; seminar teachers had been given a structure for presenting the material in a handout from Bridges and the required curriculum guide content by way of the seminar readings and discussions. During the weeks of the seminar, many participants chaffed at this preordained end goal although no one openly rebelled. This unspoken but clear direction to a given end product reinforced the idea that there was a "right way" to teach a writing course. The freedom given to participants had most to do with a teacher's individual teaching style and the fact that anything could be modified *as long as the participant could justify modifications from mainstream composition theory and research.*

Analyzing the class structurally, I found that the TBW seminar was designed to "convert" current-traditional teachers to a version of the process model, described by Bridges as the whole language, writing workshop. This classroom model advocated student-generated writing topics, in-class student/teacher conferences, extensive use of writing peer response groups to critique multiple drafts of student papers, and portfolio evaluation. Additionally, teachers were encouraged to share their writing with students, to publish student writing (on bulletin boards or in school newspapers or class "books"), and to institute informal and formal evaluation of their classroom effectiveness, using observation, writing apprehension scores, and so on. All of these modes and activities were derived from research and from the theorists being studied in the seminar, and Bridges's seminar structure clearly illustrated a convergent theory model of teacher training as defined in my introduction.

After participating in this seminar, teachers were expected to change their own writing classrooms, to move from the current-traditional, teacher-centered classroom model which they each would hold to some extent, Bridges thought, to the student-centered model, described above. Equally, by the very fact of their enrollment in the doctoral program, these teachers were open to change. Who changed, how much, and why, were the questions I hoped to explore. I should note, however, that before I completed this structural analysis and written description of the TBW seminar, the overwhelming focus of Tom Bridges and the pedagogy seminar on teacher change had not been clear to me, nor was the convergent theory instructional model well defined. Such definition occurred later, after I discussed my findings with Bridges and completed a second bibliographic search in the area of writing teacher training.

I found a few teacher trainers, like Ruszkiewicz (1987), and theorists, like Brooke (1987, 1988), suggesting the new model that Bridges was already, and intentionally, implementing.

Pedagogy Seminar Setting

The seminar met from 3:30 to 5:30 P.M. five days a week for five weeks, with two Fridays off. Class convened in a traditional air-conditioned classroom building with blackboards, a large teacher's desk at the front, and moveable chairs with writing arms. Throughout most of the sessions, participants sat in relatively the same positions, chairs facing toward the instructor at the front, unless they were directed into groups. On a few occasions class convened in a circle. A few teachers made it a habit to change their location, but overall the positions they took remained relatively stable. Generally, I sat in the last row, center, at the back of the classroom.

By the second week, many seminar participants, often the instructor, and I met in the lounge of the building before class and gossiped, joked, and traded information. One learning log group also met there twice a week. At first, a few teachers avoided the informal gathering and always proceeded to the classroom to read or review notes. By the end of the term, however, on certain days, nearly all seminar participants would meet there informally for as long as twenty or thirty minutes before class.

Tom Bridges's Expectations for the Pedagogy Seminar

Tom Bridges expected teachers in the Teaching Basic Writing seminar not only to become believers in the whole language, writing workshop classroom but also to become devoted and hardworking doctoral program members and professional educators. Bridges judged the seminar effectiveness, in part, from that perspective also. The need for participants to shift roles, develop public professional identities (scholar, researcher, teacher), and manage conflicting allegiances in these areas was woven into the fabric of the rhetoric program and deeply imbedded in the instructor's own expectations.

During one interview, Bridges articulated his own evaluation process for the Teaching Basic Writing seminar.

Bridges: Um. I know that at the end of a course like this I'm sometimes pleased and sometimes disappointed in what they actually turn in as final results and I think that factor will be there again—that there'll be——

Researcher: Okay. That's one question. My last question. How will you decide if this class has been successful or not? How will you know that?

Bridges: Uh. I think my first and foremost criteria is an affective criteria. This class will be as successful as we come together. You know, that ratio, if we can come together and really feel like a unit working and, sure, having our disagreements and what have you, but if I get that sense at the end of the semester that everybody's here and we're humping and we're helping each other and what have you. Uh, then the class is a success. And I don't particularly care, like I said before. I don't want them to be able to reference. I want them to be able to teach. So if I have that sense of this class then I'm pleased because I think the vast majority will be people who will go back and do neat things in their classrooms.

Throughout the course of the seminar, during after-class interviews, Bridges discussed the teachers' affective development and his overall evaluation of class progress. He would refer spontaneously to moments where things worked or to participants who were exhibiting change. He was continuously evaluating and monitoring ongoing class activities.

Bridges: They [things in class, the TBW seminar itself] went just okay today. You know my marking system in conference is plus, zero, or minus? This would be a zero [class]. It wasn't a plus or minus. Uh, but we'll see if the Applebee arguments get people ready for the changes that we're going to have to do.

At the end of another class he responded more optimistically, "Well, they're all going to be our [change] agents out there [in the teachers' institutions]." Built into Bridges's theory of teaching was an implicit belief that participants would change. He looked for this change as the class progressed, and during the last weeks he could point to positive results.

> *Bridges:* I had the sense that some of them were beginning to see them-selves in that classroom . . . it looked like some of them were beginning to picture themselves not creating the classroom out here and that's what our job is but rather seeing themselves in that classroom beginning to ask questions as someone in that classroom rather than someone just outside looking in. So I suppose that's the next step that you'd expect to see.

This seeing-the-self-as-process-teacher step was important to Bridges's sense of class success, and he monitored every participant for the smallest signs.

> *Bridges:* I thought she had, not today, but the end of last week, a lot of good things to say. And she's joining in and saying things that were de-cent and insightful and getting ready to think about changing her class-room. Oh I was going to say, did you catch Julia on that [statement about changing her next class]? Well, that's testimony, right? In front of the congregation here.
>
> [*later in the same interview*]
>
> *Bridges:* Oh yeah. I made a note when I was up front [of the class] of the people talking from inside and not outside. I sensed that in Alice, Ken with a nod and quick agreement with Alice.
>
> *Researcher:* There are people who have assented?
>
> *Bridges:* Well, yes, who seem to be asking questions like, from the inside now. It's like when you learn anything. At first, from the outside, you're playing with the potter's wheel, and now you're trying to throw the pot. The questions you ask and the ways you ask them are different once you become an insider to it. I just had a sense today that maybe for Helen and I'm thinking about Roger now.

Throughout the seminar, Bridges looked for, and felt he saw, changes—teachers developing as insiders both in the doctoral pro-gram and in the classroom—changes that were confirmed in the seminar teachers' own evaluations of TBW. Bridges was able to pin-point many instances of teachers re-seeing their classrooms and teaching practices. As participant-observer, I, too, was able to record instances when teachers acceded verbally to new viewpoints in pre-class and learning log conversations and during in-class seminar discussions; and in most instances, the final curriculum guides showed well-developed, theory- and research-based, whole language writing workshop classrooms, and participants received "A" or "B" grades from their professor, Tom Bridges.

From the teachers' viewpoint, the Teaching Basic Writing seminar was successful. In learning logs, interviews, and surveys, teachers reported that they were pleased with the class format, the instructor's engagement with and presentation of materials, and their final class projects. Life in TBW was not easy, however. During the course of the seminar, teachers struggled with difficult readings, with a perception that the instructor might be advocating a different method (student-centered teaching) than he was himself using in the classroom (more teacher-centered or structured teaching), and with a frustration at the difficulties of developing an "ideal" model for teaching writing when their strongest classroom memories were of real-world struggles with institutional and classroom constraints.

By the end of the Teaching Basic Writing seminar, though, most teachers felt they not only had resolved some of these issues but also learned a great deal by engaging just such issues. All of the teachers reported in interviews that their final curriculum guides were 80 percent to 99 percent "real" (written for themselves and not just for Tom Bridges and class purposes) and that they were looking forward to teaching again. Subsequent case studies allowed me to explore how effectively these positive affective and practical gains translated into a teacher's own classroom practices.

Teacher Change Through a Pedagogy Seminar

Before developing case studies, it is necessary to review the very real development that teachers experienced through their participation in the pedagogy seminar, Teaching Basic Writing. First, seminar readings were carefully sequenced to present discipline-wide concerns and arguments (i.e., the nature of the composing process, the usefulness or ill effects of direct grammar instruction, and so on). In that sense, readings greatly supported Tom Bridges's goal of leading teachers to develop an informed pedagogy—a whole language writing workshop—when they returned to their institutions. At the same time, class readings were all well respected works, representative of the best research currently being done in composition. This also was in keeping with the instructor's goal that teachers should develop research-based arguments for their classroom practices.

Second, instructor lecture was a strong point of the TBW seminar. In their learning logs, many participants said that they liked to listen to Bridges. In lecture mode, the classroom had all the attributes of a successful, traditional graduate seminar—and some of the drawbacks. Although they were appreciative of the materials being presented, participants exhibited less active and more traditional student behaviors during lectures—reading learning log notes instead of listening, doodling, talking to neighbors, falling asleep, and so on.

However, the greatest confusion about the lectures developed due to the conflict between behavior appropriate to graduate seminars and the topic being covered: how to run a student-centered classroom. For some participants, this confusion was highlighted by Bridges's own practice of using metateaching comments, "Okay, now we'll play graduate seminar. I'll sit here and you talk." Or (his remarks at the end of a formal lecture in sentence combining), "Wasn't that boring?" It seemed to me, as classroom participant-observer, that part of the teachers' experience in converting to a new teaching theory or methodology included: (1) the desire to find a single right answer—an impulse that sometimes could lead teachers into overapplication of class premises, i.e., teacher-lecture is always bad or you should *never* (ever) teach grammar; and (2) a feeling that all classes, whether at the doctoral level or at the freshman level, should follow the same model if both were based on the same "philosophy" of teaching.

Third, in-class group work was used primarily in the pedagogy section (middle third) of the seminar and was sometimes skipped due to Bridges's own sense that material needed to be covered more quickly. In learning logs, group work was recorded as a very successful learning activity but also, at one point, as the vehicle for some of the most disturbing learning experiences of the class, when several teachers performing mock conferences were disturbed by their classmates' critiques of their performances. Many teachers wanted to have more group activities, while some thought that the group work was fake or nonproductive. Parallel to this, both in logs and in interviews, teachers recorded their own lack of success with classroom group work, their own fears of implementing group work, and their own sense that they and their graduate program peers didn't participate well in group work, competing more than supporting. In this study, several teachers seemed to lack models of collaborative work in their own previous educational histories and to be unwilling to collaborate freely in the competitive doctoral program environment. The role of collaborative groups in teacher training classes and teachers' previous attitudes toward such activities are clearly areas worthy of greater investigation.

Fourth, teachers did a small amount of in-class writing. When asked to draw and describe their own models of the composing process, several balked at being asked to perform in class. When asked to write a memo to the instructor about their final project, many were taken aback. They performed these tasks but did not express much enthusiasm. They seemed as reluctant as any freshman writing student to write on demand for a teacher. However, when the task was less evaluative, as when they were asked to tell stories about their teaching pasts, they performed the in-class writing and sharing with a great deal of enthusiasm.

The whole area of teachers' attitudes toward their own writing performance was only touched upon in this study, and the results suggest a need for much greater investigation (see also Berkenkotter, Huckin, & Ackerman, 1988). Teachers exhibited familiar apprehensive behaviors and their own strong attitudes toward writing (writing in general and writing as doctoral participants in particular) surely affected their seminar learning and their writing classroom teaching.

Fifth, out-of-class learning logs and learning log groups were major focus points of learning for most teachers. Learning logs helped seminar members with time management, allowing most to stay current with readings and discussions and to come to class more fully prepared than they might otherwise have been. Learning logs also helped teachers assimilate reportedly difficult readings. Several teachers planned to use the logs as study guides a year or more later, when they began reading for comprehensive exams in the area of composition theory. Coding of logs by T-unit for teachers' subjects and focuses allowed me to identify three major response patterns (see Appendix); teachers generally took one of three roles toward the class materials. Some were Scholars, those who focused on class issues and readings—often second year doctoral students; some were Practitioners, those who focused on their own teaching and/or home institutions and/or general attitudes about the teaching profession; and some were Analysts, those who focused on several subjects—readings, teaching, and their own activities or identities—writing entries most often for purposes of self-analysis.

Several teachers, primarily those with Analyst and Scholar profiles, used the log most often as an arena for practicing for the seminar. It became obvious that learning log groups helped these teachers to feel safe and to develop a doctoral participant persona. Log groups also allowed teachers to question the seminar and to resolve conflict through peer discussion. In groups and in the logs, teachers critiqued the seminar, responded to the instructor's teaching style, expressed fears of failure, and made commitments to the teaching model and plans for the future. Learning log groups functioned as model group learning experiences. There were some of the predictable flaws of group work (overly dominant members and an occasional tendency to get off task), but log groups also supported teachers' class learning in every cognitive mode—reading, speaking, listening, writing (Bishop, 1989).

Finally, end-of-term writing projects, most often the curriculum guide and rationale, contributed in a major way to the teachers' development in the seminar. Writing activities have long played an important role in teacher learning in the training classroom. Those participants who completed curriculum guides and rationales for the TBW seminar thought the activity was an essential vehicle for synthesizing their learning. Additionally, for the instructor's purposes, the guide resulted in at least a promise of "conversion," due to its implicit contractual nature, and it seemed to function as a regulating mechanism because of its literal cost in time and energy for the participants. They would not lightly abandon a document that took so much time to write and which *did* address their immediate teaching concerns for the fall semester.

The best summary of the value of the pedagogy seminar came, of course, from the teachers. In a final learning log entry, one offered this superficial yet concise wrap-up. "A real response to this course would take more paper than I have in this notebook and more time than I have in 1987. But for now, this sums it up: I learned, I had fun, I met lots of nice folks, I read lots of good stuff, and I'm a better teacher. That's about what I wanted out of the course." Reading over this and other teachers' remarks, Tom Bridges mentioned that these were precisely some of the results he had hoped for from the class. And certainly they match some of his expectations, mentioned above, that teachers leaving the seminar should "go back and do neat things in their classrooms" after having worked hard in the seminar, come together as a learning community, and developed a research-based curriculum. How they implemented this curriculum is, of course, the focus of the next five chapters.

2

Susan, a Pre-College Level Teacher of Writing: The Challenge of the Structured Process Classroom

I have these immature freshmen who are used to being led by the nose. I mean, there's a bad side to this; they will do what I say. And they're not concerned about where all of this is going, really. So if I start by saying—if I start by saying we're going to go through this process—they're going to look at me and go what? They're used to sort of suspending the self to the teacher's authority and saying, okay, we're going to do this little piece today, and tomorrow we'll do this little piece—it is hard to find a balance there.

—Interview with Susan, fall 1987

A COLLEGE WRITING TEACHER WITH FOURTEEN YEARS PREVIOUS teaching experience at both large and small institutions, Susan was also a trainer of secondary school teachers and a member of two professional organizations (Conference on College Composition and Communication, and Western College Reading/Learning Association). She subscribed to three journals related to writing (*College Composition and Communication, College English*, and *Journal of College Reading/Learning*). Susan kept a teacher's journal and wrote letters to friends and family. She also wrote with students on some class assignments, developed presentations and papers every semester, and wrote daily memos or business letters and an occasional grant proposal as part of her administrative duties. In these details, Susan's teaching and writing profile was strikingly close to that of the average doctoral program participant at Gatton University, although she appeared to write in more modes and more often than some graduate students.

In the early 1980s Susan changed employment, moving from a position in a Writing Center at a large state university in California to a classroom teaching position at a four-year college in Oregon. She said she was "happier in a classroom setting (rather than in a lab), where I can engineer the *entire* reading/writing process." In this remark, two of Susan's pedagogical concerns are highlighted. Susan was interested in issues of instructional scaffolding, in how she might need to (and often did) "engineer" the writing/learning process. She was also concerned with students' reading development and wanted to learn more about reading theory.

Early in her doctoral program enrollment, Susan described her strength as a teacher of writing as her ability to design "cumulative assignments in which students use/rethink earlier papers." She described herself as skillful at "responding to student papers through comments." Susan saw herself as a teacher predisposed to change, and incentive for change came from student input and from her own growth. And finally, Susan listed some of her own difficulties in teaching writing. "My comment sheets seem to overwhelm students. Some students want lists of criteria for papers, complaining that they don't know what I want despite all the prewriting activities we do." Since she did teach a secondary level methods course for training writing teachers, I found that Susan had read fairly extensively, perhaps more than any other new doctoral participant, from the literature of composition studies.

Susan and the Doctoral Program

Susan's overall response to the doctoral program and the pedagogy seminar, Teaching Basic Writing, was positive. She valued the program and respected the TBW seminar instructor, Tom Bridges.

However, mixed with this positive response was an articulated resistance to that course in particular—a resistance that stemmed, perhaps, from her own familiarity with course materials due to her teacher-training experience. In an early interview she said, "Now the second term [summer session] where I'm more in an area where I think I know something about, I may be a little bit more testy." Susan explained that during the first session, when she enrolled in the research methodology course, she was more willing to accept and learn materials because that was an area in which she had little background, especially in quantitative research. However, when she enrolled in a class like Teaching Basic Writing, for which she felt more prepared and better grounded in the literature, she tended to resist, somewhat, what she felt to be Tom Bridges's slightly dogmatic approach to instruction.

As Susan discussed the elements of the Teaching Basic Writing seminar that caused her to experience some resistance, she said she believed in the model Bridges was presenting—the whole language, writing workshop approach—yet she was unable to adopt, wholeheartedly, the seminar focus on a research-justified "best" model of teaching writing. Here, her own background as a teacher trainer—one who was aware of the competing theories available in composition studies—may have kept her from taking a believing stance in Tom Bridges's convergent theory pedagogy seminar.

Equally, Susan may have felt that Tom Bridges, although an excellent instructor, was somewhat closed to discussing the validity of the model he was presenting in class. In a sense, she was describing the problem of how to be an autonomous learner in a highly organized learning situation—how to balance "student freedom" with "teacher direction." And trying to achieve this type of balance was of great importance to Susan in the writing classes she taught.

Susan's Concerns

Like the teachers in Munby's 1987 study, "Metaphor and Teachers' Knowledge," all case study teachers, including Susan, had recurrent themes of interest and concern in their teaching, and they often used metaphors when talking about these issues. Although Munby was not able to explain all aspects of metaphorical language in teachers' representations of their work, he was able to show that "it is reasonable to believe that the metaphors used reflect something of how the speaker sees or constructs professional reality. If the metaphors are used persistently, then the case for their representing a construction of reality becomes more compelling" (p. 380).

As did some of her doctoral program professors, including Tom Bridges, Susan often talked about parts (pieces) and wholes (the big picture). Like most writing teachers, Susan was a collector of good teaching practices, but, like most doctoral participants, she also believed (or learned to believe) that the parts must equal a greater whole, one which unified theory, research, and practice. She often mentioned her desire to create a big picture from the pieces of her teaching past and her learning present.

The concept of parts influenced Susan's class choices in the Teaching Basic Writing seminar. For instance, during the early weeks of Teaching Basic Writing, she decided not to write a curriculum guide for freshman or pre-freshman English because, she believed, she had previously developed an effective course. Instead, for her final project she chose to develop a sample course for tenth-grade English, as a model document for the English Education majors she trained in her teacher training course. That choice allowed her to "put more pieces of the model that we've been discussing into the curriculum guide at the tenth-grade level than I can at the college level."

Although Susan often used parts/whole comparisons to discuss her desire to develop a full view rather than a partial view of a theory or classroom or learning experience, parts/whole metaphors were used in a second way in the doctoral program and occasionally in her own discussions. In the doctoral program, such metaphors describe two different views of learning. In the first, whatever is to be learned is a stable artifact, *knowledge*, which can be imparted or ordered from an accretion of parts and passed on to a student who is viewed as a receiver of knowledge, an "empty vessel" waiting to be filled. This view of learning (bottom up; parts-to-whole; atomistic; skills-centered) can lead to a skills approach to writing, one in which students learn to write strong topic sentences in order to develop clear paragraphs. Writing clear paragraphs leads to clearly organized, schematic essays, and so on—the developmental sequence always going from the smallest part (word, sentence) to the largest (essay or discourse) (Shuy, 1981).

In the second view of learning, what is learned is the result of a process, a dipping into the whole; and the whole, although it can be described by its parts, is always greater than the sum of the parts (top down; holistic; constructivist; writing as discovery; writing to learn). This view of learning leads to a whole language classroom where students learn to read and write, not by stringing together parts but by immersion in the ongoing and complex stream of knowledge-making: by writing whole discourse and reading that discourse and revising that discourse and discussing that discourse with peers. Parts, when they are discussed, are discussed as adjunct concerns to the whole (Harste, Woodward, & Burke, 1984; Knoblauch & Brannon, 1984a; Shuy, 1981).

These metaphors and these arguments were often taken up in Gatton University rhetoric program seminars where, generally, *writing to learn* theories were championed against *empty vessel* learning, or where the *holistic* versus the *structured* approach to teaching writing might be discussed. It was never clear that Susan ascribed to either viewpoint exclusively.

Parker (1988), in a review of research into teachers' theories of writing instruction, describes a study by Barnes and Shemilt.

> "[It] suggested a continuum of teacher's views of knowledge and its relation to writing in classrooms. They called the poles of this continuum transmission and interpretation and offered composite profiles of the views of typical transmission and interpretation teachers. Transmission teachers believe that knowledge is objectively contained and divisible into public disciplines, which, via lectures and assigned readings, the teacher transmits directly to passive students. In contrast, interpretation teachers value the learner's personal meanings, and therefore, define teaching as creating circumstances in which students use language to transact with curriculum material, which in turn means they are actively constructing knowledge in their own right. (pp. 21–22)

Susan seemed to move between points on this transmission/interpretation continuum, depending on which professional identity she was activating: doctoral student, writing teacher, writing teacher trainer, and so on. As a doctoral student she might express interpretation teaching values; yet as a teacher of pre-freshman writers, she sometimes expressed transmission teaching values *and* interpretation values. In doing this, Susan was not alone. In fact, Susan's use of parts/whole metaphorical language seemed to indicate a desire to forge theoretical and practical unity in her classroom(s). Susan's metaphors of parts and whole pointed to a complicated set of instructional problems, decisions, and concerns. It is not surprising that such terms entered a doctoral participant's vocabulary; it is noteworthy to mention though how thoroughly they entered Susan's vocabulary.

Susan and Instructional Scaffolding

Another educational metaphor that Susan used was that of "engineering" a learning experience, a term directly related to the concept of educational scaffolding. The discussion of educational scaffolding grows out of the issue of parts and wholes. Those who advocate scaffolding or "engineering" in the classroom have both strong supporters (Applebee, 1986; Hillocks, 1986) and detractors (Harste, Woodward, & Burke, 1984; Knoblauch & Brannon, 1984a); others find themselves almost distressingly in the middle of this pedagogical argument, plagued by the issues raised (Bartholomae & Petrosky, 1987; Bizzell, 1987).

Scaffolding, as presented in the Teaching Basic Writing seminar, was *not* a desired classroom model (just as interpretation teaching was preferable to transmission teaching). In fact, Tom Bridges was strongly against the idea of instructional scaffolding and often ridiculed the term. However, he did not appear to realize how pro-scaffolding Susan was, although she mentioned the issue in her final class project.

Some of Susan's interest in and defense of educational scaffolding came from her understanding of the views of other program professors whom she believed supported a more structured methodology. Some came from the Teaching Basic Writing seminar readings, particularly the Applebee article, "Problems in Process Approaches: Toward a Reconceptualization of Process Instruction" (1986). In the TBW seminar, this article was intended by Bridges to help orchestrate a guided rebellion. Seminar participants were expected to *reject* Applebee's advocacy of a "structured process approach" as the solution to the problems Applebee cites (i.e., that process instruction is not taking hold or does not appear to be effective in American writing classrooms). Such a rebellion would spur participants on to develop ideal, but also real and *practical*, writing process classrooms that instituted unstructured workshop approaches. In Susan's case, the Applebee article appeared to be taken at face value and not as Devil's advocacy or a rallying point, and she used it to support her already well-developed belief in the efficacy of instructional scaffolding. Rather than modify her belief in instructional scaffolding to adapt to Bridges's presented views, Susan selected the most useful material or pieces from TBW and from her other classes to put together a stronger model of a structured classroom.

Discussions of instructional scaffolding versus natural process are dualistic (you can have one or the other, but not both) and contentious. An individual engaged in these discussions, as reflected in classrooms and in the composition studies literature, may be the same person who is trying to resolve extremes of transmission and interpretation teaching (Parker, 1988); Kroll, in his 1980 essay, tries to mediate between two versions—what he calls the nature and nurture models of instruction—and suggests a moderated position somewhat similar to Applebee's. In fact—scaffolders like Hillocks (1986) who advocates an environmental approach, Kroll (1980) who advocates interactionism, and Applebee (1986) who advocates structured process and attempts to redefine Hillocks's research—think they have taken the middle ground and resolved the either/or argument of pieces/whole, bottom up/top down. But proponents of a natural process, or the whole language classroom, see them as more conservative and traditional than they would like to be seen, as new packagers of the current-traditional and parts-based instructional paradigm, as partaking of a "smorgasbord" approach to assembling pedagogy without a philosophical basis (Knoblauch & Brannon, 1983; 1984a).

Like the advocates of moderate scaffolding, doctoral program participants would often rebel against the need to take sides, to make choices, and often asked if these viewpoints couldn't be reconciled. This feeling of unease with the either/or nature of the discussion surfaced in Susan's comments. Although far more of a scaffolder than any teacher studied, she had an innate dislike for class structures or forms that might lead to scaffolding. Susan voiced a dislike of what she called "formulaic response" in the classroom. She did not see instructional scaffolding as leading to formulaic responses. She advocated teacher engineering of the larger classroom activities (a reading leading to a paper topic leading to a sharing of student papers) rather than teacher engineering of the smaller classroom parts (worksheets and skills activities), if such a distinction can be made.

Susan's commitment to and interest in "engineered" classrooms was not then directly attributable to her TBW experience, although it may in part have been attributable to her wider doctoral program experience. Her attitudes in this area were somewhat illuminated by her attitudes toward students in general and writing process classrooms in particular.

Susan and Writing Students

As a teacher of pre-freshman basic writers, some with second language backgrounds and some with learning disabilities (diagnosed and remediated in high school), Susan was extremely sensitive to individual student need. Due to her previous Writing Center experience, Susan appeared to favor individualized instruction over collaborative instruction. And it might be argued that an individualized approach mandates a directive or "intrusive" teacher somewhat more than a collaborative approach, such as the writing workshop classroom advocated strongly in the Teaching Basic Writing seminar.

Throughout the interviews, Susan related her concern for her students as individuals. She felt they had sometimes been poorly taught by colleagues who had "the old idea that everybody should be able to do their own thing" in the classroom. She felt that she should be close to her students and help them develop a sense of responsibility. However, she did not label her students as ESL or as learning disabled and therefore needing a structured classroom. Rather, if she labeled them at all, she tended to categorize pre-freshman level students as needing directions repeated, as needing to be held accountable, or as being passive or along for the ride. She believed they saw her class "in terms of English classes they've had before." They were "not very good consumers of their own instruction," and they suspended "the self to the teacher's authority."

Viewed as *pre-freshman* students, Susan's students came out in a somewhat unfavorable light. These were students who were playing at school, whom she viewed as individuals who could clearly benefit from a more rigorous, individualized classroom in which the teacher engineered their learning until, by the end of the semester, in preparation for Freshman English, the teacher could "begin to wean them. If I have these same kids in regular freshman English next term, you know, I can hold them accountable. I can say, you know how to do this. You're going to do it outside of class now, right?"

This view of students as somewhat passive, perhaps even as vessels waiting to be filled with firm instruction, is counterbalanced and perhaps even contradicted by another set of teaching beliefs that Susan expressed. She believed, in spite of material presented by Bridges in Teaching Basic Writing, that good process instruction *was already occurring* at the high school level.

Since Susan believed high schools and colleges were implementing process instruction, she had other important mandates for her classrooms: teaching reading and teaching academic discourse. In conflict with this assumption was Susan's belief that some of her students' problems in class grew directly from their treating her class like just another high school class. Also, overall, she didn't think *one* writing class could change a student that much, or that old schemas change readily. She said, "Most basic writers are going to need a year sequence anyway, if not more." In spite of this, Susan didn't voice a strong need to reinforce their high school level process instruction with intensive college level process instruction.

While stating that her students probably already had a process background, Susan could still expect they would rely on her too much for implementing the process and just pretend to agree to a process model to get through her class. And she didn't believe that any model or theory would fit all student needs, so she would have to "start from a perceived student need or student perception of what's happening." If this were true, she would then have to rely on the self-report ("perceived student needs") of students she viewed as fallible or manipulative.

Susan probably would not have been open to enrollment in a rhetoric doctoral program nor open to change if she hadn't registered many of the paradoxical or conflicting viewpoints traced above. Keeping these viewpoints in mind, it is now useful to look at her writing class during fall 1987.

Susan's Home Institution and Writing Class

At the time of this case study, fall 1987, Susan was teaching at a small four-year college in northern Oregon. As stated in the catalog, the college intends to "provide a Christian liberal arts education of high quality to a diverse group of students." Originally hired on grant monies, though now on a regularly funded track, Susan had developed the college's basic studies program and conducts all of the pre-freshman instruction in English.

The course which was studied in this research was titled LA 93 Writing Lab, a four-credit course meeting four hours per week for the nine-week college quarter. The course description reads, "Instruction, practice, and evaluation of basic writing skills. Emphasis on improving fluency, vocabulary, command of sentence structure, punctuation, and paragraph development. Required as prerequisite to English 101 for students scoring below 34 on TSWE." Fourteen students originally enrolled in the class, and eleven filled out surveys at the end of the quarter.

Class Assignments

In Susan's class, students were asked to complete four essays and one revision, in-class activities and sentence combining, paragraphs and drafts, and a midterm and final. Class grades were computed on a point basis (that is, fifty possible points for essays, fifteen points for paragraphs and drafts, etc.).

The first two essays for the course were examples of what Susan calls "cumulative assignments," a practice she used before and after the TBW seminar. Students were given readings, participated in in-class brainstorming sessions before writing first drafts, and took their papers through a sequence of peer-critiqued drafts. In some cases, students wrote short paragraphs comparing their papers to other students' papers on the same topic. In a letter to me, written fall 1987, Susan described a cumulative assignment this way.

Here are all drafts leading up to the final essay turned in October 26. As you may be able to reconstruct from the syllabus and sets of drafts, students first wrote an in-class draft (Oct. 7) after brainstorming individual topics on "The Discipline of Nature, Culture, and Force" (see attached reading). Peer evaluations were completed the next day (see peer evaluation attached to first draft). Students then revised and added to their drafts, resubmitting them on October 12. Students read at least three classmates' drafts and wrote a page long comparison or contrast of their paper with the additional papers they had read. I then gathered all these materials, read them, and returned these drafts with my comments dated

October 14. Third drafts came in October 19, and were returned with teacher comments (dated *October 22*) after groups writing on specific "disciplines" met during class on October 21. Final (fourth) drafts were turned in *October 26* (see teacher comments + grades attached to these final papers).

First and second paper readings were taken from materials Susan had used previously and, she believed, successfully with other courses. Third and fourth essays offered students new choices. For these essays, students used the Bridges assignment generator, which was passed out and described in the summer TBW seminar. Essentially, the assignment generator is a topic, writing type, and audience heuristic. To use it, students alone or in groups list possible types of writing (autobiography, dreams, editorials, etc.) and types of audiences (self, parents, a movie or TV star, etc.), and then students discuss what they know about about different topics, the types of writing those topics could be formulated into, and possible audiences for those papers. Students end by listing one to several possible paper topics, types for writing, audiences, and so on— developing their own class writing schedule.

Writing Evaluation

Susan's description of her students' work on the "Disciplines" paper, as described in her letter quoted above, outlines her paper evaluation methods. In this case, students wrote a minimum of four drafts of papers. Although she had students revise, she preferred to call revisions "additions," to encourage her basic writers to expand their material. She felt they, too, often viewed revision as a reductive process. Her evaluation method included student review of student work and teacher review, leading to writer's revisions rather than immediate teacher grading. In her first reading of a student paper, Susan wrote a cover sheet with summary comments, like this one.

Chris,

For your comparison paper due Monday, you could continue the draft about laundry/baseball *or* compare your essay with other "laundry" papers written by Robb Gulick and Souk Ngonethong. *I like* the comparison draft you have started.

Typically, Susan pointed out where the student could go next, complimented and supported the writing, and refrained from marking directly on the student's writing. In keeping with her interest in developing student readers as well as student writers, she directed Chris to the work of others in the class.

For the next draft, Susan responded by filling out a formal cover sheet with five categories: (1) Development of Narrative/Description; (2) Definition/Explanation of "Discipline of Nature, Culture, or Force"; (3) Comparison/Contrast with Other Students' Papers; (4) Sentence Style/Mechanics; and (5) Organization/Focus. Again, she rarely—if ever—wrote directly on the student's paper.

One of the greatest changes in Susan's teaching style occurred in this area of teacher direction and evaluation of student writing. As she explained in an interview:

> I think the one thing I became a believer in this summer has more to do with the student investment in the writing at the starting point. Uh, I still think, as you can see from my comments, I still tend to be a very intrusive teacher, as saying, well . . . "with the raw material you have now, you could do this, you could do that, or you could do this." But I think I do that *after* they come up with their first or second draft, rather than from the beginning.

The student's final draft of a paper utilized the same cover sheet and comment categories, numbers 1 through 5 above, but included a point grading; Susan assigned a number achieved out of a possible ten points for each category (i.e., 8/10 points for Organization/Focus) and ended with points and a grade: for example, 39/50 "B −." There were a few editing marks on the final papers but relatively little teacher commentary or correction; all comments were placed, instead, on the cover critique and grade sheet.

A Typical Week
During a typical week in Susan's class, at least 60 percent of the class took place in whole group, teacher-led, discussion or in direct teacher lecture. Because this was a four-credit class, a certain amount of group work was relegated to the one-hour, one-credit, weekly lab portion of the class. During the two hours of non-lab class meetings which Susan video taped for me, class activities

were clearly organized and directed by her. Students followed Susan through a discussion of samples as she wrote out sentences on the board. She then had them work in pairs and consulted with each pair about their progress. As she did this, she continued to stay near the chalkboard and to note material on the board for the pairs. Susan described her work with students this way as group brainstorming. A majority of the video tape, then, showed Susan in this light—directing the whole group in a class discussion and directing pairs of students as prepared class handouts were reviewed (30 percent of class time). About 15 percent of class time was devoted to in-class writing.

Reviewing class video tapes, I noted a number of student questions aimed at clarifying directions. That is, students would listen to directions (or appear to) and then immediately ask for the same information again. Quite patiently, Susan would repeat the directions. When asked about this, she replied, "Oh that's very typical and that's what students seem to want. I seem to do more of it every year." Asked whether this problem might be due to their lack of English language fluency, the ESL or EFL background of her students, Susan said she didn't think so. When asked if she believed this constant questioning about directions might be a result of a scaffolded class—one in which the teacher structures the learning experience—she replied that she thought it more typical of private college students than of public college students. She felt they didn't bother to listen, that they were treating the course more like a high school course than a college course.

Much later in the interview it became clear that Susan was still considering this point—that she had wondered about the efficacy of her own structuring. She discussed changes she wanted to make in the future. "Instead of writing instructions coming out of my mouth [I intend, in the future, on] getting them to come out of a partner or someone else. But that's something I'm trying to change so they're not so dependent on me. As you were saying, this kind of teaching can create a monster sometimes as a student becomes more and more dependent on you, instead of less."

Reviewing Susan's out of class activities, paper reading took up a majority of her time (60 percent). Although she didn't mark directly on the papers, Susan always read papers carefully, which was in keeping with her often discussed dislike of "cold" reading during short, in-class conferences. She preferred to master the contents of the paper before a conference. Teacher/student conferences took up a relatively small proportion of her time, either in or out of class (15 percent), possibly due to the small class size and the one hour each week of lab time that allowed for individual work with students. Finally, preparing class materials took up the final 25 percent of her time out of class.

The following activities or techniques were important instructional focuses in the Teaching Basic Writing seminar:

- Bridges assignment generator
  (or encouraging student-generated writing topics)
- peer writing groups
- sentence combining
- editorial board
- student journals or learning logs
- in-class student/teacher conferences
- teacher sharing his/her own writing
- publishing student writing
- formal measures to evaluate the writing classroom

Use of these activities and techniques was seen as supportive of the whole language, writing workshop classroom, as developed in that seminar. I review them across all case studies.

Susan reported that she used the *assignment generator* during the second half of the class, and in a modified way. She used *peer writing groups* very little. She pointed out that because the class was so small it functioned as a small peer group (although clearly led by her); however, students worked a great deal in pairs, and she was pleased with this work.

Students used *sentence combining* regularly; fall 1987, for the first time, sentence combining activities were relegated to assignments outside of class or to tutor-assisted lab work. This new use of sentence combining indicated a major change of focus, for previously sentence combining had been a major in-class activity. Susan felt it was no longer possible to do the other things she wanted to do in class (for example, having paired students read each other's papers) *and* sentence combining, so she was considering dropping sentence combining exercises entirely.

Susan liked the idea of the *editorial board*, having students with strong usage skills proofread and review final drafts of student papers (as had most TBW teachers), but she had not yet used it; she planned to use it in the future. Susan did not use student *journals or learning logs;* she believed they were too formulaic. She used *in-class conferencing* very little, because a cold reading did not let her do justice to a student paper. She did not *share her own writing* with her class. She did not *publish student writing,* although she hoped to in the future. She did not *use formal measures to evaluate student progress* (such as writing apprehension scores, early and late diagnostic essays, and so on) except as gathered for the research project.

Students in this class generally confirmed this class picture. However, they listed reviews of English grammar as used several times, while Susan listed this as an activity never used. Similarly, student perceptions of usage instruction were that it was used several times, but Susan listed this as an activity that was used only once. Susan listed class lectures as used several times, whereas students listed it as a frequently used technique. Finally, Susan listed studying models of well-written essays or reports as something that was used only once, whereas the majority of the students listed it as having been used several times or frequently.

In contrast to the teacher's perception, the students' perceptions were of a slightly more teacher-led, traditional classroom. However, as noted earlier, there were strong and consistent overlaps of perception that the class focused on peer reading, multiple revision, and extensive drafting of papers. Although Susan was pleased with the class as a whole, some of her end-of-quarter teaching concerns echoed those she had listed as she began the doctoral program. "Why do some students just stop and they don't really revise, they don't push forward. Do I need to do more publication? What do I need to do with these students." She added, "For a couple of students, there's not a whole lot of change between the drafts, despite my suggestions, despite everyone else's and that's the motivation factor—that's one thing I'm struggling with." She continued her discussion of motivation by considering that she, as a teacher, might need to intervene more, not less, in the case of basic writers. "And just telling students to write, just because they go through the motions, doesn't yield results—particularly with the weaker students, so we could call this sort of hands-off sort of approach really quite elitist, I'd say. You know, it's the very thing that works really well with upper middle-class students, etc. etc."

The quarter ended, successfully by teacher and student accounts; still remaining for Susan, though, were questions concerning how much teacher "engineering" should go on in a classroom and how a teacher could motivate students to take control of and responsibility for their writing.

Discussion

Susan began the Teaching Basic Writing seminar confidently. Although she was predisposed to change, she also felt secure in her pedagogical knowledge concerning writing, due to her previous teacher-training and classroom teaching experience. If there were large areas in which she needed new information, she believed those areas were, primarily, reading theory and quantitative research.

Susan also had preconceptions about the applicability for her students of the type of whole language, writing workshop classroom that Tom Bridges intended to inculcate in his students (the teachers in the Teaching Basic Writing seminar). As she began that seminar, she considered herself perhaps more process-oriented than Bridges presumed the class as a whole to be. Susan felt that writing process classrooms were more in evidence in the high school curriculum than Tom Bridges or the research he presented indicated (although she could, at the same time, speak somewhat disparagingly of those same students). Additionally, she felt that her own pre-freshman English and freshman English classrooms were already quite process oriented.

Susan's self-evaluation may have been slightly inaccurate, like those of the teachers in Anson's informal study (1989); Anson found that teachers' perceptions of their own response styles were quite different than their actual practices. "Teachers often create idealized images of their own instruction (including their response styles) which suggest to them that they no longer need to participate in ongoing instructional development. These images are often quite at odds with their actual practices" (pp. 358–359).

Because of her preconceptions, Susan could be viewed as somewhat resistant to change. In her fall 1987 pre-freshman English classroom, for instance, she did not appear to fully utilize several cornerstones of the classroom model developed in the Teaching Basic Writing seminar: student journals, teacher in-class conferencing, sharing her writing with students, and publishing student writing. Susan generally organized her class as a teacher-led, developmental or structured classroom, although she did have a very strong and effective drafting cycle and did use evaluation techniques that supported the process classroom (reader-based responses aimed at improving writing clarity rather than teacher corrections of lower order grammatical concerns).

Viewed from the perspective of the pedagogy seminar and Bridges's goals for teachers, Susan changed perhaps only slightly from her previous methods. She did withhold her intervention, more than she had previously, and she did find that student-generated topics, through her use of the Bridges assignment generator, led to a greater, and greatly desired, student investment in writing tasks. When viewed from Susan's perspective, then, the classroom appeared much improved in the areas listed above, and she was satisfied with her quarter's work.

Swanson-Owens (1986), in a study of curricular change, reminds us that we must look at change from the researcher's *and* the teacher's perspectives.

> In my attempts to explain these teachers' responses, I use the phrase "natural source of resistance" to suggest that these outcomes identify discrepancies that are appropriate given the presence of particular mismatches between outsider and insider meaning systems. Indeed, teachers' responses seem "resistant" to the extent that they violate outsiders' expectations; at the same time, they are "natural" or appropriate if one assumes that they reflect teachers' commitments to effective practice as they know it. Discrepancies between these teachers' perspectives and my own should therefore not be construed as instructional "errors" committed by these teachers but rather as places where the implementation process runs the risk of breaking down. (p. 72)

It would seem that Susan's classroom did not change radically due to the Teaching Basic Writing seminar because she did not intend that it should change in those directions that Tom Bridges most emphasized. She felt much less dissonance between her teaching practices and the material presented in TBW than the instructor, Tom Bridges, might feel for her, or than did other teachers in other case studies. However, Susan's classroom did change, from her perspective particularly, in the area of teacher intervention.

In the Swanson-Owens study (1986), a high school English teacher and a high school home economics teacher used new instructional practices in a very pragmatic way, one that "reinforced old patterns of instruction" (p. 80), and for "reasons that reflect[ed] when 'conditions were right or appropriate' for them" (p. 94). In the same manner, Susan gathered materials relating to her concerns about instructional scaffolding and continued to organize her class around that concern. When she did drop older practices (sentence combining) she did so primarily to respond to time constraints which were very real in the quarter system.

The Swanson-Owens study, as well as a study conducted by Perl and Wilson (1986), point out that teachers' preconceptions about their students have a great deal to do with instructional decisions. Perl and Wilson summarize their three-year study of writing process instruction in primary and secondary classrooms with the following observation.

> We became interested in the ways teachers construe and communicate their views of their students' competence to their students. And we began to think that how teachers interpret what they see in front of them determines how they act and how they teach.
>
> If, for example, teachers see in their students competent, capable human beings, they seem to act in ways that naturally enable their students to explore, to grow, to stretch themselves beyond their own limitations. If they do not, if, as a result of classroom problems or their own assumptions, students appear to them as incompetent or incapable, no technique or approach they use appears to be particularly effective. For teachers, in subtle and often unintended ways, communicate their unspoken views to their students. (p. 258)

In somewhat the same way, Susan's views of the abilities of prefreshman students seemed to set her instructional agenda. Although she viewed herself as an interpretation teacher by preference, she viewed her students as requiring a certain amount of transmission teaching. Because her students acted too often like high school students, needing structure and guidance through academic situations, she looked for teaching materials that would enable her to scaffold learning in her classroom. At the same time, she became frustrated by students who asked her for easy answers—for instance, how to write essays in ways that would please the teacher.

Additionally, Susan's background with individualized instruction may have kept her from engaging more fully with the development of a collaborative classroom. Again, due to her view that her students didn't know enough about academic discourse, she wasn't willing to turn them loose in collaborative situations. In thinking this way, she may have been overlooking the very ability she complained of in her students, their ability to "play" school and to try to please the teacher. It would seem Susan's concern with teaching academic discourse was bound up to some extent with her expectation that her students would—and undoubtedly did—have trouble with academic conventions. Because of those concerns, as she studied TBW seminar materials, Susan focused on finding ways to solve this problem, as much or more than she focused on reconceptualizing her classroom as an arena for developing student writing fluency. The latter reconceptualization might have offered some solutions to the issues that concerned her at the end of her course—concerns that students weren't motivated and engaged.

In fact, Susan appeared to avoid reconceptualizing her classroom. Originally, she was going to write a curriculum guide for her freshman classroom, but she couldn't get going on the project. She did not start writing her final TBW project until she abandoned that paper idea and decided to write, instead, a curriculum guide as a sample for the high school teachers she trained, feeling that she'd be able to implement more of the seminar suggestions at that level. In essence, Susan saw the materials presented in the TBW seminar as most appropriate for her high school teachers. By the time students had reached her freshman and pre-freshman level classes, she believed they had already experienced a process classroom in high school and that she was under the constraints of teaching academic discourse. She even described her freshman level course as different than that conceived of by Tom Bridges, as needing to be a course in writing across the curriculum.

It is possible that Susan's strong interest in dealing with academic discourse came from her sense of responsibility for the entire pre-freshman program at her institution. She had designed the pre-freshman course and said she was unpressured to follow any particular teaching strategies or methods. However, as the only instructor of pre-freshman English, students passing out of her classes without adequate preparation for freshman English would, no doubt, seem to reflect poorly on her teaching.

Recent theories of schema building can perhaps provide a general cognitive model that explains how and why Susan assimilated the material from the seminar in the manner that she did. In "Schematic Bases of Belief Change," Crocker, Fiske, and Taylor (1984) posit three models for schema change: (1) a bookkeeping model in which change occurs incrementally; (2) a conversion model in which change is radical and sudden; and (3) a subtyping model in which change occurs as a branching out in which new subsets are created to store incongruent information. Of these models, the subtyping model may give an idea of how Susan processed TBW seminar materials. To subtype, Susan would create a new category and mainly *store* her learning. She would be saying, in effect, "Should I need to create a whole language, writers' workshop model classroom, here is how I would do it and where I would find the information, *but* that model does not fit my situation." In fact, throughout the interviews, Susan registered a distrust of models or theories, even while trying to put together the whole picture of composition studies as a participant in the doctoral program.

Crocker, Fiske, and Taylor's review of schema research also suggests that persons who view themselves as experts may be more likely to reject new information than are persons who view themselves as novices. They explain that the cognitive schemas of experts are more complicated and entail more organization; therefore, "for an expert, change has higher costs than for a novice" (1984, p. 209). It may be possible that Susan's previous, wide reading in the field of composition studies made it harder for her to accede to the convergent theory model presented in the Teaching Basic Writing seminar. In her readings she had come across too much conflicting or "disconfirming" information that made her reluctant to accept the seminar direction. At the same time, her reading, while wide, did not appear to have occurred in enough depth to help her immediately resolve certain instructional questions, to totally compose her own "big picture."

It should not be forgotten in this brief overview of a long and complex instructional chain—Susan's participation in the doctoral program, the Teaching Basic Writing pedagogy seminar, and Susan's own fall writing class—that her college writing class was evaluated by the students, and by Susan, as successful. Although as researcher, I could see areas of resistance and nonimplementation of TBW activities, I had no reason to doubt Susan's or her students' evaluations. What is useful to note is the extent to which a teacher's previous instructional and educational background and her current teaching concerns influence how readily she will assimilate information from a pedagogy seminar.

3

Rosalyn, a Pre-College Level Teacher of Writing: Grammar and the Process Classroom

I see this is heavy stuff [the whole language, writing process classroom]! Still, it's worth a try because too many of the transitional students (basic writers) at my school seem to be caught in a revolving door of English classes—they keep failing.

—Rosalyn's learning log, summer 1987

WHEN SHE BEGAN DOCTORAL WORK IN RHETORIC DURING THE summer of 1987, Rosalyn had five years previous college level teaching at the same institution from which she received her M.A. degree in Communications. A mid-size urban university in the southeast, her school is the "third largest black institution of higher education in the nation." In the fall of 1987, Rosalyn directed her university's Learning Skills Center *and* taught three courses, including pre-freshman level writing. Rosalyn's classes were composed predominately of minority students, and she was interested in helping her students adapt to or enter into standard English-speaking communities by helping them become "bi-dialectal."

Rosalyn was a member of three professional organizations (College Learning Association, Conference on College Composition and

Communication, and National Council of Teachers of English), and she subscribed to three journals, each put out by one of those organizations. She wrote letters, memos, and monthly reports for ROTC sections of English writing workshops that she also taught. Although her teaching and writing profile was close to that of an average doctoral program participant, she had less classroom teaching experience than some doctoral students (five years compared to the average of ten years), and she wrote less often than many. She confirmed this picture when she described herself. "Because I do not write as often as I should, I would appraise my writing ability as average."

During the Teaching Basic Writing seminar, Rosalyn's modest appraisal of her own writing ability seemed to explain, in part, her strong interest in sections on developing models of writing processes and in discussions about writing apprehension. These interests connected to her already strong sympathy for her struggling pre-freshman writers. Like Susan in the previous case study, Rosalyn began teaching in a writing center environment at her institution's Language Skills Center. She felt her experiences with individualized instruction helped her "relate to the basic writer. I have the insight to go beyond his/her mechanical problems and assist with content and organization first."

Rosalyn listed a variety of techniques that she used to teach writing (collaborative learning, peer tutoring and evaluation, writing multiple drafts, using writing models), and she professed the influence of a process approach, due to writing workshops she had attended. These had been led by composition specialists such as Edward P. J. Corbett and Harvey Weiner. The ROTC writing classes Rosalyn taught were special, ungraded writing workshop sections that allowed her to participate in the workshop experience without her usual, often noted, program constraints. However, her current-traditional English department was even then redesigning its curriculum at the instigation of a new chairperson, and Rosalyn was involved in that curriculum revision process.

Not surprisingly, then, Rosalyn saw herself as someone who "sometimes" changed her teaching from semester to semester. She would "look at what is most effective and the current research. If they are applicable to my situation, then I 'go for it.'" However, constraints on her teaching surfaced in many responses as Rosalyn considered the questions of how much grammar she should teach, how much innovation was possible in her situation, and even how she might be judged by her colleagues. "Sometimes I get very informal when teaching my basic writers. Although it works for me, I think that most of my colleagues do not believe in getting too close to their students," she wrote on an early survey form. Even while she worked at an institution that supported change, through workshops and curriculum revision, Rosalyn dealt with an undercurrent of traditional expectations and responsibilities.

Rosalyn and the Doctoral Program

Rosalyn came to the doctoral program because she was interested in the summer enrollment option that would allow her to continue teaching, and she was particularly interested in the opportunity to take the Teaching Basic Writing seminar itself. "And when I saw basic writing, I found that useful, we call it transition, I guess it's the same as basic writing, and I find that even though I guess I do things that work, I needed to get the theory behind it to see, you know, what I could add to my little repertoire."

Rosalyn found the doctoral program demanding and sometimes wondered if she could keep up. She termed herself a different type of learner than her peers in the dorm—one who had to read, reread, and assimilate material slowly and carefully, and one who might have to stay up until 3:00 or 4:00 A.M. to do so. However, she enjoyed what she was learning, found it applicable, and seemed determined to succeed at what she had taken on.

In the Teaching Basic Writing seminar, Rosalyn responded favorably to Tom Bridges as an instructor, although she was much more hesitant about her position in the class at the beginning of the course than at the end when she noted, "For some reason, and I'm not sure where it comes from . . . I do feel more confident in the class [laughs]."

Like several of the teachers, Rosalyn's desire to learn theory was always tempered by a yearning for practical classroom applications, "I still thought, I need more hands on, more you know, I guess, pages of suggestions . . . things I can try." Nevertheless, for Rosalyn, the Teaching Basic Writing seminar seemed to have successfully fulfilled her own goals at program entry by allowing her to learn more writing process workshop methodology. She said of herself, before the TBW seminar and after, "I guess I was a semi-process oriented [teacher] [she laughs]. Now I hope to become a completely process oriented teacher."

Rosalyn's Concerns

Unlike Susan, Rosalyn relied less often on particular metaphors to describe students or learning, but she did have several traceable themes and concerns that reflected her ability and her intention to implement Teaching Basic Writing seminar material in her writing classroom in the fall of 1987.

Because her background was similar to the background of her students, Rosalyn seemed to view her students as peers, as individuals with strong potential who needed to sort out educational goals, to understand dialect constraints, and, in essence, to learn to make it in an academic environment. Although she once referred to students' immaturity, she seldom viewed them as other than extremely capable, to the point of considering her fall 1987 writing class exceptionally mature. "In fact I wonder how most of them [her students] got into transitional [basic] English because most of them seem to be very good writers."

Rosalyn showed a consistent attitude of respect for her students' abilities and a concern for her students' growth. She portrayed herself, convincingly, as caring deeply about empowering her students, even while she realized that not all teachers at her institution felt the same way. "I've found that many of my co-workers don't want to teach basic writers. So I seem—I enjoy that area; I guess when the light goes off in their head or in their eyes, whatever, and they've connected everything." Rosalyn made it clear that she enjoyed seeing students make connections; their eyes would light up or their grades would improve. Her own memory of struggling with her writing and her sensitivity to how students might view a new class practice, like mirroring, made her careful about what practices she would adopt or adapt. Rosalyn's exploration of the issue of mirroring shows how thoroughly she considered her students' possible responses.

And I'm not sure that I'm going to use the mirroring. I mentioned this in my journal. I for—I just don't think—I thought about Shirley Brice

Heath's ethnography with the black kids, uh, in that they have problems with the school talk as opposed to the home talk. I'm not sure that the average black student is going to feel comfortable with my repeating in other—paraphrasing, mirroring what he or she has already said—I can just hear. They probably won't say it, but I can just hear them saying, "Is she crazy? What's her problem? You know I *just told her that*" [laughter].

Early in the Teaching Basic Writing seminar, Rosalyn had reflected concerns about how students perceived her in the classroom and how they would accept a new technique like mirroring. But she decided to try that technique and many other activities. As her fall 1987 semester began, she explained, "If something isn't working I don't feel it's just the end of the world, you know. I can just go back and apologize or tell the students, well this is all new for me too. So I think I've changed that way." By the time Rosalyn had finished teaching her pre-freshman writing class in fall 1987, concerns about student judgment had lessened. Although she was aware that students would find a technique like mirroring puzzling or weird, she was, overall, much less worried about losing face with students, and she mentioned how she had explained openly to them that in teaching the whole language, writing workshop classroom, she was trying something new. And in interviews, she described this new freedom to share her thoughts with students as at least partially a result of her new methods.

Standard English and Grammar Instruction

At the same time Rosalyn extended her new classroom ability to "let go" as a process teacher—making metacognitive teaching statements, cluing students in as to activities and class directions, sharing her writing and her hopes and fears for the class—she also continued to be aware of what she saw as her cultural responsibility to help students understand their dialect, the issue of dialect switching, and the prevalence of standard English in the workplace. Because of her own sensitivity in this area, her concern over the place of grammar instruction in the basic writing curriculum (which was a concern of many TBW seminar participants) surfaced early and continued through all our interviews.

During TBW, Rosalyn discussed issues of standard English in her learning log. "Many of my students do not use what one colleague calls 'English for the marketplace' standard English, so I think that they should be exposed to written and spoken standard English as much as possible. Then they can make an informed choice I hope." And Rosalyn described her own schooling experiences as similar to those of her students. "A few years ago, or maybe several years ago, you know I couldn't shift back and forth with my dialect, you know before I went to college, and I know how important that is, you know, to do that. At least to a degree."

Given this background, it's not surprising to find that Rosalyn constantly voiced her concerns and thoughts about the efficacy and need for grammar instruction in the writing workshop classroom. When Rosalyn began the doctoral program, she indicated she was aware of research showing that direct grammar instruction was not efficacious in the writing classroom (Braddock, Lloyd-Jones, & Schoer, 1963). At the same time, she was concerned with adequately preparing students for proficiency exit tests which they were required to take at her university. Additionally, Rosalyn was under pressure from students who would ask for grammar instruction and who sometimes saw such instruction as providing an easier (that is, more familiar) class and from colleagues who expected grammar to be taught in the classroom.

Rosalyn's concern about how much and what kind of grammar instruction was appropriate for *her* students was reflected in her final Teaching Basic Writing seminar class project, a curriculum guide and rationale for her fall 1987 pre-freshman writing class. She intended to make it a real (usable) document, especially as her semester would begin immediately after she completed her summer courses. In the guide, Rosalyn mentioned a new plan for addressing grammar instruction. The plan included noting down student errors and pulling samples for discussion from their papers for class work sheets. This was a change from her former practice of using prepared drill sheets, and many of those sheets, she joked, would have to stay unused in her files. "So, I guess that probably all those [grammar exercises] that I have in my cabinet I won't be able to use so many of them [laughter]. It probably—I'm probably going to have—I probably will have to—I'm just not sure how I'm going to handle it I guess."

When grading the final curriculum guide, Tom Bridges challenged Rosalyn on the point of grammar instruction, asking, "Have you seen these common problems in their writing before? From past years? How do you find common grammatical problems?" This section of the guide, combined with "discussion" as a prominent activity, caused Bridges to view the guide as somewhat traditional and teacher-centered. Bridges's evaluation bothered Rosalyn, who felt she was trying to balance her newly found beliefs and methods with a healthy respect for institutional constraints. In' interviews, Rosalyn mentioned feeling challenged by Bridges's remarks, and she determined to show him that she could and would produce a student-centered workshop class.

Rosalyn's decision to change her methods of direct grammar instruction was part of her deliberate introduction of a student-centered curriculum, but her decision wasn't without worry or concern for her. Relying on her reading of theory and research (Braddock, Lloyd-Jones, & Schoer, 1963; Hartwell, 1985; Williams, 1981) and on class discussions, Rosalyn realized she would have to first abandon her set grammar instruction. In her fall 1987 writing classroom, she used a few handouts from the class text and a few of her older handouts that discussed usage rules; however, she downplayed this element of grammar instruction, relying instead on current student samples. She also used student journals as a diagnostic tool, keeping a private list of student strengths and weaknesses. Still, as the semester progressed, Rosalyn believed she needed to spend more than her allotted half-hour a week on grammar and usage instruction and review, and she did quiz students on grammar in order to prepare them for their exit test.

Although it took her longer to make class worksheets when she used student samples, Rosalyn did feel the activity was worth her time. That practice was more in keeping with her process approach, and she felt students were more alert when reviewing their own sentences. While she did not begin the semester evaluating student journals, Rosalyn explained that students asked her to start marking their grammar/usage problems in journals to help them improve. As this use of journals contradicts most of the literature in the area of freewriting and journal keeping (Fulwiler, 1987), I questioned her closely on her beliefs about marking journals. According to Rosalyn, the marking of journals was an activity requested by students—and one that she felt she couldn't ignore.

Researcher: Okay, now, uh, one thing I was interested in [about] the journals; it's fairly unusual to write in the journals, to correct in the journals, like you said you had been doing. Now how do you feel about that?

Rosalyn: Yeah. As I say, I wasn't doing that at first. And I would just make comments. Like trying to look at all the theory, I would write long comments and answer them and all this. And I guess I just had people who really, I guess they liked the comments, but they really wanted some other feedback. So after they wrote about that for some time . . . I talked to the class about it and they all thought it would be helpful for them to see where they were, how they were making progress, so then I did put little checks.

Researcher: Now do you think that was because you weren't [writing] as much on their papers, so they felt the need for teacher evaluation somewhere else?

Rosalyn: Well, yeah, I think they had just been programmed by other teachers that everything they passed in has to be checked—or you don't have any comma splices this time, or what have you.

Researcher: Now, did the journals—did you see improvement after that? Did they enjoy that?

Rosalyn: I thought—yes. After I was letting them see. After I put little checks, whatever, and, so—I don't know. I guess for some it would be that it just made them feel, I guess, deflated or whatever. But those students [in her fall 1987 class] were a little mature for freshmen. They wanted—so I felt that was my job—if it was going to help them.

When asked if she would correct journals another semester, Rosalyn said she probably would offer students that option from the beginning. She thought that students responded well to those journals (which she also found an invaluable teaching activity because of content), and she explained her decision. "As I said, I guess I was trying to do everything by the book, and I found that you've got to make some adjustments to fit your particular situation." Rosalyn believed she had produced the student-centered writing workshop classroom she would be proud to have Tom Bridges see. She also pointed out that the basic writers perhaps didn't believe in themselves enough and that maybe if she had more time, perhaps a yearlong class, she could have found more student-centered ways to present grammar.

In terms of grammar instruction, it appeared at first that Rosalyn had made a radical shift away from methods used in previous years ("But then I said, 'Well, if I'm going I might as well go all the way' [develop grammar sheets from student writing instead of using textbook worksheets]"). This shift was followed by a return to more grammar instruction than originally planned, but using a greater variety of methods (student samples, journals, quizzes) than she may have used before. The increase in time spent in this area as the semester progressed could have been directly related to the students' upcoming exit tests. This pattern of major innovation, followed by a recalibration that pulled a liberal technique back to a slightly more conservative application, occurred not only for Rosalyn, but also for other case study teachers (notably Peg, in chapter 4).

Reflections on Change

Throughout the interviews, Rosalyn offered many comments about how it felt to change her techniques and made a few observations about teacher change in general. Those comments illuminated her attempts to redefine grammar instruction in her class and illustrated her own change process. For Rosalyn, the process of change elicited a mixture of affective responses: caution and optimism and a sense of challenge and professional validation. Taking the Teaching Basic Writing seminar seemed to consolidate and accelerate a process of change that Rosalyn already was undergoing voluntarily. That is, she came to the doctoral program needing to read and to incorporate more theoretical information into her writing classroom. These needs were engendered by her relatively light self-directed reading of professional journals, by participation in writing workshops with composition specialists, and by her department's review of its composition sequence.

Rosalyn was optimistic that she had the materials at hand to produce a strong writing workshop classroom, but she was cautious about how much change she, personally, could oversee in a single semester. For instance, she instituted successful peer critique groups and in-class conferencing. But she decided to wait at least a semester to introduce the portfolio system because it would place a lot of time pressure on her during final grading periods, due to her heavy administrative and class loads and the large number of portfolios those classes would produce.

She was also more confirmed in her understanding that direct grammar instruction would not produce permanent changes in her students and that the whole doctoral program supported her learning in the area of literacy studies. Rosalyn began to institute new ways to provide the usage instruction she felt her students needed. In doing this, she was productively challenged by Bridges's approach that asked her to justify all her classroom activities from research and from classroom needs.

Finally, participation in the doctoral program and in the Teaching Basic Writing seminar gave Rosalyn strong professional validation. When she returned to her home institution, she viewed herself, and was viewed by her colleagues, as a composition expert. She shared her curriculum guide with other faculty, with her department head, and with her dean, and she described how she took stronger stands when she worked on committees and when she reviewed curriculum changes. She put it simply. "I think when you've taken the course [TBW seminar] it makes it more legitimate with your peers."

It would seem that Rosalyn was a teacher in a state of flux. She had not taught so many years that she felt sure about her classroom, yet she had taught enough to know that classroom behavior (that of both students and teachers) can be improved through teacher study and reflection and through monitoring ongoing activities. Rosalyn's enrollment in the doctoral program seemed particularly well-timed to support her natural growth without asking her to "unlearn" too much material. That she, like all teachers, had to "unlearn" a certain amount can be seen in her struggle to discover a new and effective way to include grammar and usage instruction in her classroom. Keeping these directions in mind, it is now useful to look at Rosalyn's writing class, fall 1987.

Rosalyn's Home Institution and Writing Class

Working at a mid-size southeastern university, Rosalyn teaches a large number of "transitional" students—those enrolled in one of the two pre-freshman level courses called Writing Laboratory or Language Enrichment classes. The course which was observed in this research project was the latter, ENG 053, Language Enrichment, a one-semester course that meets for three hours each week but offers no credit. The course is necessary for those students whose test scores indicate they need it to prepare them for the three-credit freshman English course. The course description for

ENG 053 reads, "Designed primarily to enhance the student's enthusiasm to develop proficiency in language skills by reading selected materials to strengthen concepts and by writing and speaking to enrich effectiveness of expression." The mandatory generic syllabus, distributed for all sections of this course, records the aim of the class, "to prepare students for successful writing performance in college-level English courses and in all courses requiring skills of written English expression." Fifteen students filled out first-week forms, and twelve students completed last-week surveys for this study.

The English department generated a six-page course syllabus and schedule that included information on course objectives and requirements and on grading; a course outline by topics (i.e., Understanding the Word; Understanding and Writing the Paragraph, etc.); procedures for moving from ENG 053 into the second-semester freshman English class—challenging ENG 101 freshman English; required texts; and basic criteria for a satisfactory short theme. Rosalyn included a handout of journal and conferencing guidelines and continually supplemented the syllabus with class handouts in the form of usage activity sheets.

Class Assignments

Students were required by the English Department to complete at least three expository paragraphs and five short themes. They were also required to take a final examination consisting of a writing sample and an objective test of course content and skills.

Instructors had the leeway to grade based on the following criteria: class work 50 percent, final examination theme 25 percent, and final objective test 25 percent. Given the 50 percent weighting her department gave to exit testing, Rosalyn would naturally have concerns about preparing her students for this procedure.

Writings early in the semester were of paragraph length, generated from teacher assignments (the first being a summary paragraph to meet a writing across the curriculum requirement that all students be able to summarize material), responses to class readings, journal entries, and the Bridges assignment generator. Journal entries were frequently assigned and often asked for metacognitive discussion of students' feelings about conferences, their own writing, the writing workshop activities, and so on. Writing assignments later in the semester were longer, two or more pages, and included assigned forms (character sketch, letters, social/political or religious issues, and so on). All papers went through draft stages and often were preceded by individual, group, or class brainstorming sessions and/or discussions.

Writing Evaluation

Rosalyn relied on peer critiques during the early drafts of student writing. She mentioned some difficulty in prompting students to generate their own critique sheets, feeling they came up with so many possible criteria in class discussion that the critique sheets were too cumbersome. At this point, she substituted a critique sheet from a teaching text, one that was simple and, she believed, effective. In interview, she described an in-class critiquing system that I later observed on video tape.

> *Rosalyn:* They would go to the peer group first to brainstorm and start writing. The peers listened to the paper and then they read it themselves and then that's when I got it—at that point. To me, that, I thought it helped, you know, by the time they had got it to me, uh some revision had been done—I listened too. Listened to them read the paper and then uh the student and I both talked about certain areas, whatever. I tried to get them you know to see what they were. And then they went back and revised. And that's [when] I got, I guess, that last revision.
> *Researcher:* Will they be revising those papers again? Or, the incompletes will be revising them again, or———
> *Rosalyn:* Yeah. The incompletes will be revising.

A sample early paper shows a student-written second draft with no teacher or peer handwriting or comments on it. The final, graded draft had Rosalyn's marginal comments on usage. These had been indicated in the text by small checkmarks. In the margin, checkmarks were supported by statements ("hyphen not needed"), questions ("when?"), and revision directions ("not a whole thought [check handout on fragments]"). A summary comment was affixed to the end of the long student paragraph and was, itself, fairly lengthy.

> Your summary is thorough although some points seem to be secondary ideas. Some of these problems could have been cleared up during the

conference, but you missed it. Severely hearing impaired/deaf—don't they mean the same? Remember that writing multiple drafts is not just editing, which comes later. Your drafts should reflect *revision* as a result of input from your teacher and peers.

At the top of this paper was the grade of "C − − −." The writing evaluation in this typical class sample was both innovative and traditional. First, through the use of peer groups and in-class conferencing, Rosalyn withheld written comments on her students' papers during early drafts, even on the unmarked second drafts. Using oral reading of papers, she encouraged students to hear and correct their own usage problems. As a result of her doctoral program readings, Rosalyn was familiar with literature in this area (Gere & Abbott, 1985; Harris, 1986; Mayher, Lester, & Pradl, 1983) that suggests students can perform quite a lot of self-diagnosis and correction, particularly when they read out loud.

In her marginal comments, Rosalyn wrote fairly traditional responses, although she avoided the use of *frag* and other unmeaningful (from students' viewpoints) editing jargon (see Knoblauch & Brannon, 1984b; Larson, 1986). Her summary comments were also traditional and included some scolding. Rosalyn pointed out that the student had missed a conference, and then she tried to tie usage concerns to her "activity" sheets. However, Rosalyn also used the terminal comments as an arena to discuss writing process and revision.

Since this was a final draft and would probably not go through further revision, as that student was not collecting materials for a portfolio, extensive terminal markings may or may not have had much effect on improving the students' writing or writing process, if we believe researchers like Knoblauch and Brannon (1984b) and Larson (1986) who describe how often this material is unclear or is ignored by students.

For longer papers from the second half of the semester, the review process was similar. At this point, there was slightly more intervention in terms of usage comments on earlier drafts of the papers. For one set of papers that contained two drafts, the early draft had checks and usage comments, written in more terse editorial style, (*-ing needed*, *SV*, *fragment*), and a written response at the top of the paper: "Good job! Please see me about errors and another paper." The focus, even on this "good" paper, seemed to be as much or more on error analysis and correction than on explaining to the student what successful rhetorical strategies had been employed to produce a "Good job!" The final draft began with "A – " and "Good job" and had the same type of notations in margins. In the second draft, earlier fragments, -ing problems, and other usage problems had been corrected by the writer, and a few new usage problems were then highlighted by the teacher: *Pass., pl. needed, sp.* Revision of the paper content was not obvious. From this and other samples, it was not clear that revision entailed much more than cosmetic, teacher-directed correction or general, surface-level proofreading by the student.

Rosalyn spent 25 percent of her class time either leading discussions by the whole group or lecturing, activities she sees as similar. She spent the remaining 75 percent of her time in small group activities such as conferences and teacher and student in-class writing. The class video tapes showed approximately 75 to 95 percent of the class time devoted to the last three categories; there was relatively little teacher-led discussion or lecture. Rosalyn said this was different during other weeks when slightly more time was devoted to lecture. Rosalyn normally left at least one-half hour each week for grammar activity sheets and exercises.

During the classes that were video taped, students worked comfortably in groups while Rosalyn held conferences, moved around class to talk to groups, or simply monitored their work (what she called "hovering"). Students did quite a lot of writing in the classroom, marking papers in response to peer comments or moving off from a group to write alone. When the teacher intervened in a group, she would remind the group of group roles ("Who read first?").

When she returned to her conferencing corner, Rosalyn reminded the class she was available by asking, "Anyone ready to come over here?" It was clear that students were allowed to convene conferences. During these in-class conferences, Rosalyn mirrored student responses and offered suggestions for development by asking questions, "What do you think about————?" By often asking, "Anyone else ready?" the teacher prompted students to move from one stage to the next in preparing a shareable paper.

The second day of video taping (second class hour), students worked on a grammar activity sheet while Rosalyn continued to confer with students. When reviewing activity sheets, students appeared less engaged, joked more, and looked at or visited other groups; finally, some worked on the sheets alone instead of collaboratively, as Rosalyn had asked.

Out-of-class activities for Rosalyn were weighted heavily in the area of teacher conferences (50 percent of the twenty hours per week she said she devoted to this class alone) and properly reflected her concern for individualized support and counseling for students. As she observed wryly of herself during several interviews, she often didn't read enough in the literature of the field of composition studies because she gave so much of her time to her students. Of her remaining out-of-class time, 25 percent was devoted to evaluation of the types of papers described above and 25 percent to preparation, often (as in this class) to make up class activity sheets.

The following activities or techniques were important instructional focuses in the Teaching Basic Writing seminar:

- Bridges assignment generator
  (or encouraging student-generated writing topics)
- peer writing groups
- sentence combining
- editorial board
- student journals or learning logs
- in-class student/teacher conferences
- teacher sharing his/her own writing
- publishing student writing
- formal measures to evaluate the writing classroom

Use of these activities and techniques was seen as supportive of the whole language, writing workshop classroom, as developed in that seminar.

Overall, Rosalyn used a majority of the techniques and activities listed. Her use of the *Bridges assignment generator* seemed to have been somewhat confusing for the students and somewhat in contradiction to her other assignment constraints. For instance, she started the class with a summary type paragraph assignment that was intended to support the English department's writing across the curriculum responsibility and ensure that students could summarize readings in their other classes. Rosalyn later moved the class to assignments involving modes and models, as described above. Meanwhile, she introduced the assignment generator and allowed students a certain amount of topic "freedom," but not in the largest sense of creating a workshop where they were always writing about their own topics. In fact, when almost all the students chose letters as a form they wanted to write, Rosalyn worried about a student who wrote a short letter of five to six sentences and tried to turn it in for credit. She was clearly still learning to integrate student-generated assignments with perceived constraints on writing types and forms.

Peer writing groups were very successful from Rosalyn's point of view. She had used them in the past, but not often enough she believed. Although she still had questions about how to train students to critique, she mentioned being surprised and pleased at how useful their comments to each other were. She believed this supported the research she had read in the Teaching Basic Writing seminar. On the other hand, the *editorial board,* which she set up with permanent membership and used occasionally, did not seem particularly effective. In the case of final editing, peers did not seem to successfully groom each other's papers.

Rosalyn used *sentence combining,* but not in a regular format. She would talk about it in conferences and in class, and to her surprise, students, on their exit surveys, marked it as a regularly used technique. She mentioned wanting to use it more, especially for invention purposes, a use she found intriguing.

Rosalyn made extensive use of *student journals.* She regularly assigned two entries a week, collected them, and responded to them. She used the journals to help understand her class, to aid student metacognitive study of writing processes, and to evaluate usage. Rosalyn used *in-class conferencing* a great deal. She did mention that at times she would replace some in-class conferencing with out-of-class conferencing to allow time for other, necessary, in-class activities such as usage review. Although in-class conferencing was useful, it consumed large amounts of valuable class time, and as the semester progressed, conferencing was sometimes replaced by other activities, such as preparing students for exit exams.

Rosalyn *shared her own writing* with her students and believed they were impressed with the struggles she, too, had to undergo to produce a self-satisfying piece of prose. She shared her writing with this class in spite of her own hesitancy as a writer, and she said she would do it again even though it had been somewhat difficult for her. To *publish student writing*, Rosalyn asked students to prepare papers for submission to the campus magazine. However, it is not clear how far this publication activity was taken.

Formal evaluation of the writing classroom was designed into the course but was not completed. Rosalyn collected early and late diagnostic essays and intended to evaluate them for syntactic maturity, according to the plan presented in Teaching Basic Writing. Personal illness cut into her limited time and kept her from pursuing the evaluation plan, but she planned to try again the next semester.

Students in this class generally confirmed Rosalyn's observations. However, students listed class lectures as occurring frequently, as opposed to Rosalyn's estimate of several times. Students also stated that reviews of grammar and usage occurred frequently rather than "several times," as perceived by Rosalyn. Rosalyn believed she had discussed the writing process only once (probably she was referring to her formal introduction early in the class), but the students' perception was that this subject had been discussed much more often, a reflection, perhaps, of how thoroughly the process terminology had developed into classroom vocabulary.

This classroom, from both teacher and student perspectives, encompassed a great number of the techniques and activities proposed in the Teaching Basic Writing seminar, with the exception of the high proportion of time devoted to reviewing models, grammar, and usage. By the end of her semester, Rosalyn felt strongly that she had achieved many of her early goals and had produced a workshop course that was more process-oriented than her Teaching Basic Writing curriculum guide might have predicted. She still had concerns about developing peer groups and the need for grammar instruction.

Discussion

Rosalyn began her fall 1987 pre-freshman English class with the clear determination to make changes. Particularly, she felt she needed to show her TBW seminar instructor, Tom Bridges, that she could and would institute a whole language, writing workshop classroom.

By the time she had completed her summer doctoral program

courses, Rosalyn was more comfortable with her ability to succeed in the demanding program, and she was so proud of the work she completed there that she shared her final curriculum guide with colleagues and administrators when she returned to her home institution. Her participation in the doctoral program also allowed her to get a theoretical grounding she had long felt she needed, adding to her self-confidence. In an article detailing his own graduate program experiences, Snyder (1981) explained this sense. "To say the very least, the seminar and its papers provided me with an opportunity—for perhaps the first, last, and only time—to examine, in comparative leisure, the relatively ordered structures beneath what so often appears to be a chaos of classes, conferences, preps, and grading marathons" (p. 193). And this sense of appreciation for a place and time to stand back from a demanding teaching life seemed important also to Rosalyn.

Garnes (1984) claims that the three elements needed for preparing the ideal teacher of writing are the development of teacher commitment, curiosity, and confidence. The Teaching Basic Writing seminar engaged Rosalyn, who was already a *committed* teacher of "transitional" students. She also had *curiosity* and hoped to find a relatively ordered structure underlying the teaching chaos that she, like Snyder (quoted above), experienced in her own search for theory. And finally, success in the doctoral program and measurable growth in the seminar she had most looked forward to taking, Teaching Basic Writing, gave Rosalyn the needed *confidence* to take chances and make changes.

Several of Rosalyn's own personality traits and attitudes toward writing instruction seemed to predict successful implementation of new teaching practices. First, and very important, Rosalyn had a strong understanding of her students' backgrounds and needs and was deeply committed to supporting each student's growth. Perl and Wilson (1986) found that this healthy respect for students often led teachers to see themselves as conduits. "We began to think that this kind of nonteaching, this need to 'get out of the way,' was crucial for the kind of teaching we called 'enabling.' . . . The teachers all wrestled with this dilemma as they examined what it meant to use their expertise in the service of their students' growth" (p. 256).

Getting out of the way entails a certain suppression of teaching ego and a great respect for students as individuals able to learn, and

Rosalyn seemed to have a heartfelt commitment in both areas. Perl and Wilson continue to explain. "We became interested in the ways teachers construe and communicate their views of their students' competence to their students. And we begin to think that how teachers interpret what they see in front of them determines how they act and how they teach" (1986, p. 258). Rosalyn viewed her students as, if not peers, as soon-to-be-equals—students who, like the student she had been, were learning the ways of the university. She explained to them that she was a learner too and that they were all in the workshop classroom together. And she communicated her belief that they could and would be writers. In her writing classroom, Rosalyn tried to prepare the majority of her pre-freshman level students not only to pass the mandated exit tests, but also to try to test out of the required, first-semester freshman English course and into the second-semester freshman English course.

If Perl and Wilson are right, that "what effective writing teachers do, first and foremost and then over and over again, is to offer invitations to their students to become writers" (1986, p. 259), this invitation was extended in Rosalyn's classroom, partly through her clearly transmitted expectation of student success. Other researchers point out that it may be these personal teaching qualities that are as important as particular classroom models—if not more important. Stewig (1981) claims that personal qualities and relations with students are important to teacher longevity in the classroom.

Rosalyn had many personality traits that predisposed her to change her classroom. By enrolling in the pedagogy seminar and writing her curriculum guide and rationale, she also had a *plan* for instituting a full-scale writing workshop classroom. However, the development of such a classroom seemed to exist as an overlay to other, more traditional, teaching practices. That is, Rosalyn's classroom provided everything—workshop, in-class conferences, discussion of models, grammar review, and so on—and may have done so at the risk of sending a slightly confusing message to students and overtaxing Rosalyn's own capabilities.

In this sense, Rosalyn responded to every teaching stimulus: student needs, departmental constraints, her new and evolving theoretical position, and so on. For instance, due to her concern for student success, not just in the classroom but also in the workplace, she did not completely abandon old teaching practices like direct grammar instruction, in spite of her belief in the literature that claimed such instruction was not effective. Instead, she worked hard to develop broader methods for completing the same instruction so that her students would be prepared, she hoped, for exit tests and for the need to shift dialects. In the same way, she introduced the assignment generator to allow students freedom of paper topics, but she also kept topics mandated by the department or the institution.

In a way, Rosalyn was the perfect embodiment of the "practitioner" identified in North's study of composition (1987). North describes teachers as developing a "house of lore," a wide, rambling mansion with endless side rooms and back cubbyholes of teaching knowledge. In essence, he argues that teachers never abandon any teaching practice; they simply validate new materials from their practical applications and go on; old methods sink into disuse but are there, ready to be reactivated.

This image also explains, to an extent, teacher flexibility. Rosalyn, for example, had used peer groups in the past, but not successfully. She didn't abandon the concept but, instead, reactivated her old methods and improved on them in her fall semester teaching by using the groups more often and with better success. Equally, she tried the new concept of in-class conferences and felt it worked; but she put conferences aside when she decided more class time was needed for lecture and discussion. At that point, most in-class conferences were rescheduled for times out of class.

In the area of schema development, Rosalyn may illustrate a different type of response than did Susan. Crocker, Fiske, and Taylor's review (1984) mentioned three types of possible schematic responses to change, including the subtyping model, as in Susan's case study where new information may be relegated to a new subcategory rather than changing the whole schema. Rosalyn illustrated what these researchers describe as the bookkeeping model. Here, also, change occurs gradually. The default values are adjusted each time an incongruent instance is encountered. In this view, schema revision is "a gradual incremental process of minor adjustments of tuning in response to each new piece of information" (p. 206). This model explains Rosalyn's pedagogical change as a process of receiving theory and then validating it through classroom experience, as she did in the case of grammar instruction. She did not experience complete conversion or abandon direct grammar instruction in the classroom; rather, she balanced and weighed perceived classroom needs against her desire to change, and she was willing to change her methods in the sense of broadening them.

Because much of what was occurring in her own learning in the doctoral program and in the Teaching Basic Writing seminar was congruent with Rosalyn's own goals, she changed her fall writing classroom. However, like other case study teachers, Rosalyn did not entirely throw out previously used classroom teaching practices nor did she ignore institutional constraints on her teaching, and her classroom success could, in large part, be attributed to her positive ideological stance toward her students.

4

Peg, a College Level Teacher of Writing: Individualized Versus Collaborative Learning

And at what point do I say "I can't be all things to all students—mother, confessor, analyst, problem-solver, and doctor?" Maybe I should become a lawyer?

—Peg's Learning Log, summer 1987

WHEN SHE ENTERED THE GRADUATE PROGRAM IN RHETORIC, PEG had completed six years of community college teaching at a branch campus within the Florida community college system, and she was the only full-time English instructor at her branch. Having taught intensively for the last six years (five classes per semester, mainly composition), Peg commenced her graduate studies hoping to revitalize her commitment to composition instruction. Without such revitalization, she seriously believed she might need to stop teaching and look for work as a technical or business writer (or, less seriously, as a lawyer).

Peg was not a member of any professional organizations, nor did she subscribe to professional journals although they were available through her college library. She had taken several writing workshops, and one with Roger Garrison, in which he taught his conferencing methods, was particularly memorable for her. Peg wrote journals and essays periodically, as well as letters, memos, recommendations, paper evaluations, and "a rare piece" of creative writing. Overall, she wrote less often than some program participants and had mixed feelings about her writing. She said she "hate[ed] having to write as much as my students" because she was always working on evaluations of student writing. She preferred verbal communication and found that "being a writing teacher stifles my urges to keep a journal and write creative pieces." In spite of this irritation at the dilution of her own writing pleasure, due to her duties as a teacher of writing, Peg felt she was "a good writer and being a writing teacher has made me better."

Peg also had mixed feelings about her role as a composition instructor and registered a sometimes contradictory series of strong emotional reactions to her teaching and her students. She had feelings of teacher burnout and mentioned the doctoral program as a needed change and, possibly, a professional "last chance." Peg was insistent about forgetting much of her teaching past as she began the doctoral program, in the hope that she would learn new ways of teaching that would enable her to return to her teaching the next fall with enthusiasm and greater expertise.

Peg's most used teaching technique was the one-to-one conference, emphasizing rewriting. Her ideal of a writing teacher was nearly unattainable—an individual who could make the process enjoyable, who could control students and keep them from forcing a teacher to develop prescriptive rules, who was innocent and trusting about students' integrity, who had a deep knowledge of the writing process, and who could elicit the right responses from reluctant students. "[T]he whole time this ideal teacher is witty, entertaining, nurturing, and always clear and coherent in class." Not unexpectedly, although Peg had, early on, believed she could be this ideal teacher, she was "more pessimistic" by the time she began the doctoral program in rhetoric at Gatton University. Peg continued to struggle with this demanding perception of an ideal writing teacher. And, in many of Peg's remarks there was an undercurrent of irritation at teaching constraints and a longing for improved classroom relationships.

Peg and the Doctoral Program

Peg was particularly open to the possibility that the doctoral program could influence her teaching and professional life. Unlike other participants, she did not worry ahead of time about future comprehensive exams or a dissertation project. Instead, Peg saw her course work as a step-by-step process that she could engage in and leave at any time, should she feel it was not worth her effort.

Even as she began the program, she believed her participation was movement in the right direction, and she predicted, "My experiences this summer most assuredly will influence me." She explained in later interviews that the program was much more demanding than she had expected; she used the analogy of expecting it at first to be like a 7–11 store, a place she would just step into to get the learning and practices she desired. By the end of first summer session, Peg had responded to program demands, succeeded in her first two courses, and was looking forward to the Teaching Basic Writing seminar which she called the "entree" or the main course of the summer. She enjoyed her interactions with Tom Bridges. And, although she was a quiet seminar participant, Peg felt that when she did speak up in the classroom, Bridges took her seriously.

Peg observed that some of her doctoral program peers were not as content with Bridges's teaching style and course content, but she represented herself as being quite happy with the progress of the seminar, often marveling in her journal at how the "puzzle pieces" of her learning were coming together. Like Susan in an earlier case study, but much less often, Peg used as one of her metaphorical comparisons the idea of parts of learning developing into a whole understanding of TBW seminar materials. She talked most often of parts as puzzle pieces needed to prepare her final curriculum guide and rationale, and Peg was, perhaps, reflecting some of Tom Bridges's own classroom terminology, used as he encouraged teachers to construct their "ideal" curriculum guides.

Peg's Concerns

Peg mentioned in interviews that theory was secondary to her, and her professional disengagement—lack of professional affiliations or subscriptions to professional journals and relative isolation on her community college branch campus—may have conspired to keep her in somewhat of a theoretical vacuum. This changed only when Peg went to workshops which were more practical than theoretical. Looking at her continued emphasis on the affective concerns of teaching, it is clear that some of this isolation was of her own choosing.

Peg's feelings about her relationship to her students and her feelings about students as individuals and as learners were particularly contradictory. Peg wanted to get close to students but was always wary, worried that students were going to take advantage of her. "My students are notorious for weaseling out of the remedial courses they have been required to take."

Nevertheless, Peg yearned for a "true" connection to her students. She talked about "reaching" students and achieving "rapport," which was an exhilarating feeling. At the same time, she found students backing away from such a commitment or trying to pigeonhole her, seeing her (from her viewpoint) too often as an evaluator when she wanted to be much more. "I find that most students must pigeonhole teachers into one kind. Most cannot reconcile a nurturer with an evaluator in one teacher." She complained about having to switch roles in the classroom and worried particularly about providing writing evaluation which required her to be less of a friend to her students than she would like. In her learning log, she wrote with real regret that "the students can never quite forget that at the end of the term I am still the person who holds their futures in my hand. In the end I am still the evaluator and there is no way out of that . . . so any partnership these students might enter into with me is done so with reservations." And, even while trying to relate so fully to her students on an affective level, Peg realized rather poignantly that she was moving away from them in age, and as she aged and their median age remained the same, she had "less and less in common with them [the students]."

Peg's disappointment over her perceived failure to reach teaching rapport showed in her disenchantment with student habits and personalities. A slightly different classroom reality was pointed to by her metaphors. Although students could succeed if they were diligent, she often described students as "weasels" who tried to get around the teacher, "forcing" her to develop classroom rules. Peg saw bad student habits as a monolithic force that was nearly driving her from the classroom since these bad habits made her destroy her own teaching creativity. This classroom strain contributed to her classroom burnout and produced "a wall" between her and her students. She saw the composition student at one point as wall-like, too—unresponsive, a "mystifying edifice."

Her course work in Teaching Basic Writing made Peg more hopeful about her upcoming, fall 1987, freshman writing class. She felt that she had regained perspective—"students are people"—and she hoped she could retain her newfound empathy. And all the while, in learning log entries, she worried that the "student perspective" in the classroom might be carried too far and students might use classroom freedom to be weasels, undervaluing her class, trying to avoid it, treating it like a tour—in short, not working hard enough.

Peg realized the two developments that would help her maintain empathy were her newfound understanding of student writing difficulties and her intention of bringing her own writing to the classroom—sharing her own writing process and problems with students. And, indeed, those two factors resulted in perceptible change in her classroom. At the end of fall 1987, she said, "The students are thinking of themselves as writers. They're thinking about their process more. And it's wonderful. I'd never seen it before."

Peg and Change

Peg's highly affective response to teaching change can be traced in the complicated sequence of feelings that she underwent during the time period of this study—as she entered the doctoral program and enrolled in Teaching Basic Writing, and then in her fall 1987 writing classroom. Her initial high level of enthusiasm during the summer was followed by a sense of growing disenchantment and a need for reevaluation as she finished her fall semester.

As Peg began the doctoral program, she spoke of coming to teaching more by accident than by design and said that she found teaching writing a "draining task." Peg placed a great deal of emphasis on her need for freedom and creativity, yet felt a growing frustration with state-mandated proficiency testing that was slowly turning her classroom into a forum for formulaic teaching. After Florida introduced state-mandated exit testing of freshman composition students, she said, "I began to get bored. I felt like my creativity was being more and more structured because I was having to teach *to* the test." Equally worrisome, as she began the doctoral program, Peg was concerned that her brain might have "atrophied," and she later chose not to do doctoral program independent study classes because she needed structure in order to perform creatively.

Beginning the graduate program, she decided not to review her past teaching. She wished, instead, to be truly converted—to be a blank slate that would be filled with new, creative, and exciting information. As the Teaching Basic Writing seminar progressed, though, she admitted some of her previous activities for reconsideration. "You know, I wasn't half bad." Peg may have been so willing to "throw out the baby with the bath water," as she put it, because she was afraid her disillusionment with teaching reflected directly on her own teaching prowess.

As she started to write her final Teaching Basic Writing seminar project, a curriculum guide and rationale, Peg bridled against having to plan a whole class, a whole semester's work, and claimed she never engaged in such long-term planning, finding it constrictive. She preferred to view herself as a creative teacher who invented class activities on the fly. At another moment though, she described herself as "safe, a non-risker. I like to go with what I know will work, what I'm secure with. That's why this [curriculum guide and rationale] is a really big thing for me." Peg seemed to have a fluctuating and paradoxical view of herself; she was a free spirit, but one who had to be enough in control of her activities to ensure they would succeed.

As Peg looked back on her development of the curriculum guide and rationale, she explained that the fourth week of the Teaching Basic Writing seminar was a moment when she felt freed. She decided to embrace the writing workshop approach, regardless of her state's proficiency testing mandates, and not to worry about preparing students to take the test. She explained this moment as being similar to a religious experience, one she later had trouble communicating to her colleagues when she returned to her institution. Disregarding the mandates that had constricted her classroom teaching, Peg relaxed, and "everything else that I had lost, that had made me a teacher, came back to me."

Peg began the fall term extremely excited about her curriculum. She instituted a great many of the modes and activities discussed in the TBW seminar, as described below. In her new writing classroom, until midsemester, Peg experienced a joyous sense of innovation. As the semester ended, however, teaching practicalities and her original and continuing dislike of evaluating student writing (including, now, the tremendous work of evaluating full-length student writing portfolios under end-of-semester grading time constraints) had returned Peg to some of her old affective concerns. "So [she sighs] it [the workshop method]—has it's detriments and it has its benefits [and] some of those old feelings have come back."

By the end of her fall 1987 writing class, Peg intended to look once again at her *spring 1987* (pre-TBW) classroom notes, to review the materials she had abandoned completely, and to retrieve perhaps some of those materials and practices. She intended to merge her spring 1987 classroom model (pre-TBW) with her fall 1987 classroom model (post-TBW) before teaching again in 1988. She explained that she was "looking forward now to having the first, experimental, term done. And being able to, now, fine tune it, into a well-oiled, working system." At this point, Peg considered her pedagogy more directly and appeared to be considering affective states less often than at any time in her interviews. Keeping these developments in mind, it is now useful to look at Peg's writing class, fall 1987.

Peg's Home Institution and Writing Class

Peg teaches at a branch campus of one of Florida's twenty-eight community colleges. Her institution consists of a main campus, two branch campuses, and two educational centers. Students enroll full time or part time, and a large number of evening classes are offered. Peg teaches a student population that can range from a "preppy pom-pom queen" to a "harried but determined divorced mother of five." The course which was studied in this research project was "ENC 1101, a university-parallel course for students who plan to transfer to a four-year college." It is a first-semester freshman English class, and the catalog description of ENC 1101 (English Composition I) follows.

This course is designed to develop effective written communication skills for academic and professional use. It includes practice in the selection, restriction, organization, and development of topics, and reinforces the student's facility with sentence structure, diction, and mechanics. Selected writing samples are examined as models of form and as sources of ideas for the student's own writing. Conferences provide individual instruction. This course requires written compositions totaling at least 6,000 words. If used to meet the requirements of the AA degree, a grade of "C" must be attained. 48 class hours.

Twenty-four students filled out first-week survey forms, and seventeen filled out final-week survey forms.

Peg distributed a one-page generic syllabus sheet along with her own one-page, more informal, "Course Information Sheet" and a one-page letter to students. Peg's Course Information Sheet defined the general objectives of the workshop class, the portfolio grading method, and the final grade computation. Three-fourths of this sheet relayed evaluation and grading details.

The single-spaced open letter to students talked at length about student responsibilities in the workshop classroom. They would have both "responsibility and freedom," and extensive assistance from peers and from the teacher, Peg, who described herself as a "writing coach." The letter then described the uses of the class journal, which were primarily affective. The journal was intended to be a vehicle for students. "Vent your frustrations, your fears, your anxieties, and yes, the elations and joy you feel as you write."

Class Assignments

Peg was able to use her Teaching Writing Seminar curriculum guide with very few changes. In evaluating her guide, Tom Bridges said it was one of the best, if not the best, guide developed by a member of that seminar. Grades in Peg's writing class were computed from a writing portfolio (90 percent) and from participation (10 percent). Peg described the portfolio system to her students in her course letter. In this discussion, Peg blended her new beliefs about the benefits of the portfolio system (it encourages drafting and idea generation) with pragmatic, institutional constraints such as the 6,000 word obligation for composition students.

Early in the semester, assignments came from first-week list making, freewriting, and journals and from an early interview of a class-mate. The first week was devoted to gathering information, the second week to training in class modes (small group work, journal writing), and the third week to discussing the composing process, which also led into group writing and class development of writing criteria. The fourth week, students shared papers and applied the criteria, and Peg introduced the Bridges assignment generator. All class work to that point helped students develop six assignments for future writing. At midsemester, students turned in the peer interview, one assignment from the Bridges assignment generator, and an essay/letter of self-evaluation, which was considered a persuasive writing exercise.

The second half of the semester, students made out their own schedules of writing assignments, including due dates, topics, audiences, and proposed rhetorical modes. Peg intended to help order writings in sequence, from writer-based to reader-based prose when possible. The writing workshop system set up during the first half of the semester was then assumed to be in place. "Each remaining piece on the student's assignment schedule will follow the familiar routine already established in the workshop atmosphere." This schedule included students establishing goals for each piece, writing, revising, and seeking support from peer groups, from an editorial board, and from participation in student-teacher conferences.

The tenth, eleventh, and twelfth weeks of class were left clear for workshop. The thirteenth week, students prepared a piece from the portfolio for publication in a class book. The fourteenth week students prepared the end-of-semester portfolios that included first interview papers, five papers generated from the assignment generator, a writing process journal, one final piece of writing chosen for teacher (graded) evaluation, and a final letter of self-evaluation; the portfolio also included many drafts and critique sheets.

Writing Evaluation

As described above, writing evaluation in Peg's class was complex and many-faceted and grew out of the portfolio system; that is, all evaluation was directed toward student writing improvement in order to produce a successful final portfolio.

Peg responded to first interview papers after students had marked their own drafts, with squiggly underlining of sections that they liked and with Xs next to areas they were concerned about. Students also wrote a self-evaluation. Peg's responses to these often short (one to three page) interview narratives took the form of a personal, handwritten letter:

> Jennifer,
>   You approached this interview in a very creative way and were successful in capturing many of Lyn's interests. You put the reader into the setting nicely and have integrated Lyn's interests well, but I agree with your self-evaluation concerning your sentences. If you will try to vary the way that your sentences begin, I think you will like them better.
>   You really have more than enough material for several paragraphs. Then you could have an introductory and a concluding paragraph. You might also consider including more details concerning Lyn's marriage; that seems to be an important event for her.
>   You have begun your writing process and with each assignment will notice that you are getting better. Peg

This response sequence to a student assignment incorporates many of the goals of the Teaching Basic Writing seminar and imbeds some traditional teaching advice in a student-based response. Peg began by responding positively to the writing, giving an audience/ reader response, and then connecting her critique to the student's self-evaluation. By midletter, she offered some revision techniques (varying sentence beginnings, i.e., sentence combining; developing introduction and conclusion, i.e., traditional essay format; including details). Her summary sentence encouraged the student, Jennifer, to see that the writing Jennifer was doing was connected to class goals (writing process). Peg emphasized her support with a stance similar to that of a sports coach—a role Peg was interested in developing—when Peg told Jennifer that her writing would get better as the class progressed, a mini-pep talk. Peg wrote nothing directly on Jennifer's paper.

The final class portfolios ranged anywhere from fifty-five pages to more than two hundred pages, excluding journals. Length did not correlate with grade, although the portfolios that received lower grades were generally shorter. Two paper evaluation procedures were at work in the final portfolios. First, a single paper was given a letter grade, and then *all* portfolio materials were evaluated and checked off on a "Portfolio Evaluation" checklist; the result was a summary of course work and a final grade.

When evaluating a single paper for a grade, Peg again refrained from writing directly on the student paper, relying instead on a regularized critique sheet which the student had seen. The top portion listed the writer's name, paper title, and paper type. Peg critiqued the paper as having *good control, adequate, lacking,* or having *major problems* in the areas of *content, main idea* (including topic sentences, thesis, conclusion), *support, organization, transitions,* and *mechanics* (including usage, punctuation, spelling, etc.). In a space for additional comments she wrote a summary response and ended with a letter grade.

The final portfolio evaluation sheet allowed Peg to evaluate the journal with comments rather than with grades ("good specifics" or "says nothing") and then to evaluate the midsemester persuasive letter by listing the grade it received. The final letter of self-evaluation was not graded; it was evaluated with comments like "impressive—very specific," or "poor support for grade request."

Next, under a list of five ungraded pieces (essays), Peg listed the type of writing and a brief comment ("Narrative—captured a moment," or "Buddies—rough—only one draft"). These comments were followed by a series of summary grades: Midterm piece (the interview essay); midsemester portfolio evaluation; final piece (single paper selected for grading, using the critique sheet listed above) and an overall comment labeled "Development as a writer during term"; and then a final course grade after the statement, "Final Portfolio Evaluation (90 percent of final grade)."

Peg spent very little class time on lectures or teacher-led discussion. The majority of her class time was spent in conferences with students. She explained that this method was part of her philosophical base as a writing coach: because writing is personal, it requires personal attention.

Early in the semester, Peg instituted a number system which she had also used in previous years for conferencing. At the beginning of class, students picked up tags (numbered 1, 2, 3, etc.) and waited their turn for a paper conference. The three class hours of video confirmed this self-report, particularly since Peg intentionally started the camera before class began. Students came in and took numbers, went to work in groups or started individual writing projects, and the teacher met with as many students as possible, calling them up to her at the front of the room. Whole class work, other than Peg giving a few reminders to the class at the end of the period, was not observed.

During the video taping of the class, students worked at long, laboratory-like tables. These tables made it hard for students to form groups. The class was somewhat disrupted each day by the late entry of students or by dominant students who "played" to the camera or interfered with other students or groups. Clearly, class discipline was a problem, and this was confirmed by Peg who claimed the class was rowdier and less mature than her other section of freshman English.

While conferencing at the front of the room, Peg would occasionally look up and interact with the disruptive students, but not very strongly. She joked with them (semi-seriously chiding them) and then returned to her current individual conference. During the three hours of taping, she diligently held conferences and never circulated through the groups, exerting her classroom control from a position at the front. Occasionally, Peg would say, "Are we working, people?" and the class would say, "Yes." Not surprisingly, portions of the class looked like the ideal writing workshop, with students working seriously on their writing; however, other sections of the class were disruptive and unfocused and out of control, exhibiting the disruptive class "underlife" behavior discussed by Brooke (1987), which Brooke bases on Goffman's thought-provoking 1968 study of institutional behavior (that of a hospital/asylum—what Goffman called a "total institution").

Goffman's work shows the various ways individuals assert their identities. And clearly, underlife in the classroom can be both disruptive and productive; Goffman points out, "Without something to belong to, we have no stable self" (1968, p. 320). But this self is developed by the many ways we "resist" identifying with the stable institution. In this case, the underlife behaviors of some students in Peg's writing classroom impinged on the learning of other students in a negative way. That Peg could assert control was clear the few times she skirmished with these few students. That she often chose not to control them or to structure the peer groups in general was also clear from the consistency of the class atmosphere over several hours of observation.

Out-of-class activities were not broken down clearly. However, Peg mentioned that she didn't have a lot of time to prepare materials and that the workshop method, luckily, didn't require a lot of prep time. Once her critique sheets were prepared and the paper evaluation system was set up, it was self-perpetuating. The majority of Peg's time was spent in writing the evaluations detailed above in the writing evaluation discussion. This process was particularly time-consuming at midsemester and at the end of the semester. For end-of-semester portfolios, Peg estimated that she spent a minimum of forty-five minutes per student portfolio.

The following activities or techniques were important instructional focuses in the Teaching Basic Writing seminar:

- Bridges assignment generator
  (or encouraging student-generated writing topics)
- peer writing groups
- sentence combining
- editorial board
- student journals or learning logs
- in-class student/teacher conferences
- teacher sharing his/her own writing
- publishing student writing
- formal measures to evaluate the writing classroom

Use of these activities and techniques was seen as supportive of the whole language, writing workshop classroom as developed in that seminar.

Peg used as many of the techniques/activities as the other case study teachers, if not more, but she used them in different configurations. She introduced the *Bridges assignment generator* and used it as a focus for allowing students to generate their own topics and writing schedules. After her initial training assignment of a peer interview, students worked exclusively with contracted assignments from the generator.

Peer work was instituted in the classroom very early, with groups developing some of the critique sheets. However, by the semester's end, Peg was not as happy with this activity as she had hoped to be, and lack of success at implementing groups seemed evident in the video tapes. She mentioned that groups worked well together on the first interview paper and she felt this was due to the similarity of their topics. On later papers, she felt the groups were less able to critique the different paper topics and forms that individual writers generated.

Peer work seemed to develop against the background of a highly developed system of *in-class student/teacher conferencing*. By the end of the semester, Peg was able to say that one of her goals was to become an even better diagnostician of student writing, showing her continued interest in developing her conferencing skills—skills begun through her early work at a Roger Garrison workshop. The *editorial board* was used especially to help students ready their work for *class publication of student writing*, a bound and duplicated class "book," and for final portfolios. Student *journals* were used, but fell somewhat short of Peg's expectations. If not directed constantly to make entries, students seemed to let the journals drop. Most journals were evaluated by Peg on portfolio evaluation sheets as "skimpy" or just "okay" or as having "not much substance" or as being "spotty after midterm." Interestingly, those journal writers who were praised were often praised for being "candid," which shows Peg's continued interest in making connections with and getting close to her students.

Sharing teacher's writing was used once, and *formal evaluation of the writing classroom* was not done although Peg said she would have liked to. She collected early and late Writing Apprehension Scores and student statements about writing, but she didn't have the time to think about them. Reviewing these, she explained, would have required using some much needed vacation time. The vacation was seen as necessary after a particularly time-consuming final portfolio evaluation process; each portfolio required at least forty-five minutes to review.

Students generally confirmed this class picture. Some variations in student and teacher views of the frequency of activities can be explained. For instance, students marked that sentence combining was used often. Since she almost never lectured in class, Peg noted that sentence combining was never used; however, suggestions about sentence level development occurred frequently in her written comments on student papers, and student responses probably reflected this individualized teaching. In most other areas, students and teacher were in agreement about class activities.

This classroom, from teacher and student perspectives, encompassed a great number of the techniques and activities proposed in the Teaching Basic Writing seminar. Interestingly, the teacher's personal interests and teaching "philosophy" seemed to shift the focus, from a peer writing workshop model to a more individualized writing workshop model, one which relied on the teacher as coach and primary conferee. In the TBW seminar model, conferencing was an activity that went on in the background of the workshop to constructively use the teacher's time. In Peg's classroom, peer activity appeared to go on in the background of the conferencing classroom, to constructively use the students' time as they waited to talk to the teacher.

Discussion

Peg entered the doctoral program at an important juncture of her personal and professional life. She felt a strong need for change—in her classroom and in her own educational and professional pursuits. Although she did not feel she had a strong educational preparation in process paradigm techniques, she knew from her workshop experiences that such teaching materials existed. She came to the doctoral program determined to find them, particularly through her enrollment in the Teaching Basic Writing seminar.

Peg saw the doctoral program as a professional "last chance," intended to reverse her growing sense of teacher burnout. Still, she registered caution and some cynicism when faced with program demands. She was somewhat indifferent to the claims of "theory" being necessary for an English teacher, although she was pleased with what she learned in each seminar and received validation from proving to herself that her brain hadn't atrophied and that she could perform successfully in the doctoral program.

Through the course of this study, Peg seemed to be grappling with the often contradictory pictures she painted of herself and of her students. She saw herself as someone who flourished on spontaneity and who looked for teaching methods that enhanced her creativity. At the same time, she mentioned wanting to be in control of her classroom and as being more comfortable with tried and true methods.

Because she was in tune with and valued affective states, Peg wanted to commune closely with her students. In fact, a successful class appeared to be one in which students had a personal relationship with the teacher, gave a part of themselves, could be emotional, were candid, and worked hard. Peg herself reached out to students in these ways and worked very hard at responding to her classes, particularly in the area of evaluation. She held individual conferences, wrote personal critiques, read and reread drafts, and finally evaluated extensive student portfolios for every student in every class.

In creating such a demanding one-to-one relationship and work contract, Peg was, perhaps, setting herself up for an inordinate amount of disappointment. Would many students in a required freshman composition seminar freely take on such responsibilities? Clearly, at times and in certain classes and with particular peer groups, Peg herself felt that many of them wouldn't. Peg, therefore, felt somewhat abused and used when she saw students trying to avoid some of the work in her classes, becoming once again what she called "weasels."

Ideally, the writing workshop classroom should have resolved some of these problems, giving students more responsibility for their learning in peer groups. But in Peg's classroom, such a shift in responsibility did not take place throughout the whole semester. It did occur at the beginning of the semester, but then Peg began to perceive the class as being not much different than classes earlier in her career. This shift is traced in her teacher's log, kept for the first half of the semester. Here is an early, success story. "I love the fact that with this first piece of writing the students are telling me what they know. This is so logical. Before, I would have bored all of these students by telling them what they already know. . . . I keep catching myself about to tell the student what to do. I feel as if I just swore off smoking and must catch myself each time I 'pick up a cigarette.'"

Two weeks later, though, disillusionment was slipping in.

Once again, my idealism has taken a blow. Some of these students think this is still high school. If they miss a class and have an "excuse" they think it's OK.

This is still a good group; however, they are actively involved in talking about their pieces. . . . There are still many students who have not grasped the concept of accountability. This is the point where I lose patience with students. So many want the grade but are unwilling to acknowledge work is involved.

The sense of disappointment in this entry is palpable, as if students had let Peg down personally by not being dedicated. At the same time, Peg was aware that her expectation of student performance was probably idealistic. But, later in the entry, she returned to the irritating problem of student motivation, as she worried that students were not willing or able to "earn" their grades. Two weeks later she was worried about evaluation. "Writing responses to 55 students was a major task. . . . I even had to put a band-aid on my little finger of my left hand because I rubbed it so much when I wrote. The task of evaluation hasn't gotten any easier; it's just different. I still procrastinate as badly as any of my students, sometimes to the point that I must pull an all-nighter to get the work done."

Peg demanded a lot of her students; she also demanded a lot of herself through her rigorous evaluation process which was not "any easier . . . just different." And, in a way, she reacted to her own demanding schedule in the same way her students did—pulling all-nighters, procrastinating, barely getting her work done.

Peg's last entry, just before she received midsemester portfolios, showed a clear commitment to this finally less than ideal new method. "Midterm always shows a student's true colors, I think. I feel that I am more in tune with these students as individuals than I have been for years. What is exciting to me is that these students are thinking of themselves as writers. They are able to assess their own ability and progress as writers. I have never experienced that dimension in a writing class before. . . . These students are writing well and learning quickly. I am doing more individual direction than I ever did before but I expected that."

In this last entry, Peg was still trying to transcend and achieve certainty as to her system and methods. Her teacher's journal ends here, at midsemester, but the final interview with Peg showed her slightly less transcendent and, although determined to continue and fine-tune her new classroom model, aware that she needed to redesign her class. She planned to do this by reviewing her previous spring's teaching in order to see if she could replan her next class-room model based on her entire teaching past, not just on new TBW seminar material.

Peg's experience in the summer graduate program was an inter-esting instance of what I will term "intentional" conversion. In Crocker, Fiske, and Taylor's (1984) discussion of schema develop-ment relating to belief, overviewed in other case studies, three methods of dealing with incongruent information were posed. The subtyping model, which may have been in effect for Susan, allows the individual to partition off new material/knowledge, acknowledg-ing it but not necessarily using it. The bookkeeping model, which may have been in effect for Rosalyn, allows for a gradual change and recalibration as new information is incorporated incrementally in a series of minor adjustments. The conversion model posits change taking place when "salient, dramatically incongruent instances pro-duce sudden schema revision" (p. 208) such as we might expect when, say, a longtime, current-traditional teacher of English com-position takes the Teaching Basic Writing seminar. Such a teacher would find it necessary, perhaps, to totally overhaul previously held beliefs and replace them with new methods and theory.

In Peg's case, "conversion" was intentional and complete in the sense that *she always intended* to abandon old preconceptions and practices, to the point of ignoring, at first, her six years of teaching practice, in order to make what she felt, affectively, was a drastically needed change in her stifling teaching situation.

Peg needed to change because her own affective state was tied up with her success as a teacher. Hubbuch (1984) describes this sense in her own teaching.

> Teachers evaluate themselves as teachers by the performance of their students. I used to judge my ability as a teacher by the ability of my students to produce error-free, entertaining, insightful essays in a short period of time. For each student who failed to reach this mark, I put a large F in my gradebook of myself as a teacher. Lashing out at students in angry remarks like "why can't these kids learn to write?" was an ex-pression of helplessness and despair that I could not allow myself to di-rect immediately at myself: "if they can't write, it is because I don't know how to teach them to write. As a teacher, I am a failure." (p. 36)

Hubbuch continues to explain how she had to learn to "delay the time when I have to pass that final judgment on myself as a teacher" (p. 36). Peg appeared to be equally hard on herself, particularly in the area of evaluation. Evaluation is of concern to most sensitive teachers of writing, particularly because it *is* the occasion for in ducing some of the most emotional classroom interactions a teacher can have.

Peg's adoption of portfolio grading, her reading of TBW seminar materials (specifically an article by Burnham [1985] which warns of evaluation pressures), and her own self-directed reading on evaluation (Beavan, 1977), led her to develop a complex and time-consuming evaluation method that, in the end, did not protect her from the emotional worries entailed by any of the always (at least partially) subjective grading systems that can be instituted for writing classes. In her last interview, Peg said:

> I feel, I feel the student is better off although—its, grades, are very difficult, for example, like the students who got "B + " on their portfolios. I knew in my heart their portfolio, their writing, was not worth an "A" but how to justify it to them. I couldn't put my finger on and say well, this this is what makes the difference. You know, using the holistic method, you holistically know there's a difference between the "A" and the "B" but to be able to objectively put your finger on the difference is difficult, particularly in a way the student's going to understand.

In spite of her conversion to a new evaluation system that promised to be in keeping with a process class orientation, Peg was still concerned, as a teacher sensitive to her students' emotional responses, with communicating grading standards to students.

It may be that Peg, although she converted readily and designed a model curriculum guide, was less able than she thought to begin again with a clean slate or to throw out the baby with the bath water. She gradually came to feel that what she had been doing previously was okay; that she could keep some of her old classroom practices, particularly conferencing. Peg actually seemed to have developed what Poulin and White (1985) in their research into composition models called an individual workshop approach. That approach differs from the peer workshop approach advocated by Tom Bridges in the Teaching Basic Writing seminar. Poulin and White describe this individualized writing lab as being different from the writing work-shop in its "emphasis upon the individual, providing a setting in which the course instructor or a tutor works with student writers by themselves" (p. 28).

After the first few weeks of the semester, Peg's classroom seemed to move as much or more toward individualized instruction than toward active peer group instruction. This is not surprising given Peg's commitment to the in-class conference of the Garrison method and given the reinforcement she received for in-class conferencing from the Teaching Basic Writing seminar (including readings in a well-written class text, Harris's [1986] *Teaching One-to-One*, which focuses on this type of classroom support for writers). This one-to-one focus also underlies Peg's basic attitude toward writing—that it is an arduous and highly personal process. She had more than a touch of what Brodkey (1987a) describes as a romantic devotion to the image of the individual writer. Brodkey argues persuasively: "This essay presumes that those who teach as well as those who take composition courses are influenced by the scene of writing, namely, that all of us try to recreate a garret and all that it portends whether we are writing in a study, a library, a classroom, or at a kitchen table, simply because we learned this lesson in writing first" (p. 397).

Learning to direct writing peer groups in the writing classroom may help students and teachers to modify this monolithic view of writers and the writing act. But, for Peg, and for other teachers in the Teaching Basic Writing seminar, transition to the collaborative classroom was not a simple step, sometimes due to the very fact that these teachers themselves had not often experienced this method for learning. They were hesitant and sometimes confused as to how best to implement writing groups. Peg expressed this hesitance in interviews, although she was determined to use groups. Her groups worked more functionally at the beginning of the semester than at the end, leaving a class emphasis on one-to-one instruction, which in turn required a larger time commitment from Peg.

In a sense, it may be impossible, judging from what Peg experienced, to attempt "intentional" conversion to a system without doing violence to former teaching practices. North (1987) would argue that teachers never abandon their old practices and, indeed, Peg did not, in the end, seem to abandon her commitment to one-to-one instruction and the solitary nature of the writing act. It may be that converting too soon or too completely blocks a certain amount of needed introspection and analysis of past practices. In Peg's case, intentional conversion led to a certain amount of disappointment when she found that her writing and evaluating load was not changed, and neither was her essential relationship to her students. It appeared that whenever she felt she was working too hard, she was bound to see her students as not working hard enough. Because of her emphasis on the individualized classroom and because of the number of composition students she had to deal with (often sixty-five or more a semester), Peg's version of the whole language, writing workshop classroom set her a predictably frustrating task. As she reconsidered her past teaching, as her last interview showed her doing, it appeared that she would continue to develop a new version of the writing workshop model, one which would more adequately and comfortably support the changes she had made to that point.

5

Nick, a College Level Teacher of Writing: The Teacher at the Center or the Teacher at the Side

Personally, I think eclecticism is a natural result of our being experienced, thoughtful languagers in our own right, with talents and skills which make it impossible for us to adopt any teacher's system exactly and completely. Inevitably, we will find something in every system of teaching the composing process that doesn't quite mesh with our inclination, tendencies, wants, experiences, goals, biorhythms, or styles—or doesn't mesh with the wants and needs of our students. Clearly, there's nothing wrong with our not using that which doesn't mesh.

—Nick's learning log, summer 1987

NICK HAD A TOTAL OF NINE YEARS OF COMMUNITY COLLEGE teaching experience, and he had taught for the last four of these years at a small community college in western Pennsylvania. Regularly, Nick had covered up to five writing classes per semester (125 composition students) before more recently substituting two sections of speech classes for some of his composition teaching load. One of Nick's primary reasons for entering the doctoral program in rhetoric was potentially to move from two-year to four-year college teaching. He was a member of one professional organization, the National Council of Teachers of English, and subscribed to three professional journals (*College English, College Composition and Communication,* and *Research in the Teaching of English*). Nick wrote monthly letters, memos, and creative writing projects, and essays every semester for his doctoral program course work. Since he lived within commuting distance, Nick had been enrolled in the graduate program for two academic semesters (fall 1986, spring 1987), taking one class each term, before the summer under study (1987).

Nick wrote less frequently and in fewer modes than some participants and expressed strong feelings about writing, tending not to complete projects and to prefer work in progress. "I have written so many pieces, both fiction and nonfiction. Because as long as I don't finish them they have a certain liveliness about them. And, and, that may be insecurity. Maybe because once you finish it you have to send it off and see if it's worth something; but no, I think as long as you're looking that the joy is in the hunt rather than in bringing the quarry down."

At the same time, he mentioned disliking (or not yet being comfortable with) writing for his own doctoral program instructors. "I honestly believe that I write well, but not for people who are in a position to perhaps judge, with authority on their side—in brief, I'm still uncomfortable writing for my graduate profs, though I believe I'm learning to overcome this inhibition." Nick looked for solutions to this dislike of closure and his nervousness about writing to an authority figure (issues that interest him later in his own writing classroom) in the collaborative classroom and in the development of personal voice and individual writing style.

Nick noted that his attributes as a teacher were enthusiasm, tirelessness, patience, gregariousness and the ability to identify with students and determine student needs. He also felt these were some of the many needed attributes of an ideal teacher of writing. He characterized himself as having been, until recently, eclectic in his approach to teaching writing but felt he was moving in the direction of process teaching due to his two previous doctoral program courses. His most used teaching techniques were peer evaluation, student writing workshops, journal writing and discussion of entries, teacher/student brainstorming of subjects and topics, and discussion and informal grading of student samples.

Nick believed he needed to "learn to give my students more control of the process, and I need to become more of a facilitator than a teacher." As Nick moved his classroom from his previous, more traditional, methods to the writing workshop and process approach, he also considered the changes such a methodological approach implied for teachers—becoming more student-centered and less in control of the classroom; he reminded himself that the next semester he would have to "learn to do less talking. I must keep reminding myself that writing in my class is the students' process, not mine." Nick fully expected to change or he would have to "learn to call myself a charlatan."

Nick and the Doctoral Program

Nick was highly enthusiastic about what he was learning in the doctoral program. His reaction to materials was often affectively based, and he appeared to be most responsive to material he had encountered most recently. For instance, an influential book from his first summer session class, Knoblauch and Brannon's *Rhetorical Traditions and the Teaching of Writing* (1984a), was often cited in his interviews and class learning log and functioned as a touchstone or locus of comparison for most new readings.

Perhaps because he was a commuter student, Nick had a relatively distanced viewpoint from which he discussed the graduate program and other teachers. He was not seduced by program pressures to write "publishable" papers and felt it was a bit foolish of professors to expect—and of other teachers to try—to achieve such high levels of performance. He also reacted to what he believed was classroom competition. Other participants in the Teaching Basic Writing seminar often vied to "perform" well as doctoral students while he, himself, preferred to sit back and watch and enjoy Tom Bridges, whom he valued highly as an instructor and as a model teacher.

Nick used a number of metaphorical comparisons to describe his learning and to discover analogous explanations for material he was working to assimilate. He used metaphors from science fiction ("Mr. Spock from Star Trek said, I'm quoting, 'Change is the essence of being'"), religion ("Tom—thanks a ton for the baptism. I am now a devoted convert"), questing ("I have that quest, that quest requires my constantly evaluating and changing"), sports ("So if a writer's not succeeding, where else can we lay the blame but at the coach's feet"), and cooking ("All chefs use the same ingredients that we do in our kitchens. The secret is in their proportion and combination, designed to suit the chef's and his customer's tastes"), among many other categories.

Nick felt that humor was important to teachers. For instance, in his class learning log, he claimed, "There aren't many human universals, but we all must agree that two of them are our fondness for play and our therapeutic appreciation of humor. Is there a better way, then, to reach all of our students, to relieve any anxiety, or to create an environment conducive to learning than through the use of 'game playing and humor'?" And the uses of humor in the classroom were a factor in his case study. Nick also developed an analogous but slightly different version of the parts and whole metaphor found in Susan's case study, and he used it to describe his attempts to sort out the rights and wrongs of implementing new practices.

Nick's Concerns

Like any teacher intending to integrate new approaches with previous teaching experience, Nick reflected a series of teaching concerns that, in some way, mirrors the theme of parts and whole in Susan's case study. In Nick's statements, though, the process of developing a new approach is more complicated than just waiting for the necessary pieces with which he might forge a new theoretical whole. Nick registered a multiplicity of sometimes contradictory options and posed many questions. He wondered how he could balance eclecticism with a consistent plan, the right way with wrong ways or even the possibility or likelihood of finding any single way. "I had been approaching my teaching lately, eclectically, choosing this and choosing that, without ever really having defined a philosophy, and without ever really thinking about why I'm doing what I'm doing. And I think it's important to know why—I will finally, for the first time ever [after TBW], have what will be a consistent plan."

Nick talked about teaching positions shifting 180 degrees, and he mentioned that even his most recently adopted practices needed to be revised ("I can't recall exactly what I said three or four weeks ago, but I was a dilettante. I dabbled with this and I dabbled with that"). He saw that a teacher could be a dilettante or dabbler in need of reconceptualization and commitment. A teacher could "see the light" or gain understanding. A teaching position could be foggy and impassioned, even uninformed, but intuitively right. Throughout, Nick acknowledged the need to develop a coherent philosophy or theory-based practice but saw that doing so presented a perplexing proposition. "The theory for me hasn't completely come together in one solid identifiable mass for me to look at and to examine and to know." In order to perform the drastic overhaul that Nick hoped to perform in his own teaching, he felt that he, as a teacher, had to review class materials from a doubter's stance, making sure that eclecticism was theory-justifiable and the result of thoughtful consideration.

Nick found himself in a complicated position, then, when dealing with Teaching Basic Writing seminar materials. He was worried, primarily, that he may have previously been picking and choosing too freely from materials, developing an eclectic classroom. And certainly Tom Bridges's emphasis on a convergent theory, whole language, writing workshop classroom would engender such worry in a participant. Another anti-eclectic force would have been the Knoblauch and Brannon book, mentioned above, which argues against a "smorgasbord" approach to teaching writing and for teachers' developing a "philosophy" of teaching (1984a). Therefore, Nick looked for a way to build a classroom based on a coherent teaching philosophy and/or from theory, the focus of Tom Bridges's class. But, understandably, Nick had some trouble figuring out how to do this.

All too often, each theorist that Nick read was momentarily convincing but then was undercut by the next theorist he read. Thus, he was always doubtful. "I think the problem is that every time you turn around . . . what you're going to encounter is . . . a writer who is just as convincing about his or her point of view as the other writer was about his or her diametrically opposed point of view. . . . And I think some of us are so eager to define it all for ourselves that that's what becomes paralyzing. That you're saying, 'Now wait a minute. I just read this article but this article contradicted with this other article that I already believed in. So what am I supposed to do now?'"

From his doubter's stance, Nick argued that doubters were necessary so that practitioners in the profession didn't become complacent, making the field stagnant. He saw himself as resident doubter, in fact a "heretic," and felt his own graduate program instructors must be committed to having him develop his own viewpoint if they themselves were to be seen as consistent with their own teachings. However, Nick's doubting seemed to be as affectively motivated as it was pedagogically or theoretically motivated. For instance, he rejected sentence combining as a valid whole language, writing workshop classroom activity because, for him, sentence combining smacked of grammar instruction, which he didn't like.

Nick's solution to the problems of curriculum, theory, and philosophy, then, appeared to be to filter the materials at hand through his personality. And even later, when he took his curriculum guide to his class, he didn't follow it closely because he resented the control it could possibly exert over his classroom tone. Midway through his fall 1987 college writing class, Nick observed: "I started out following it [curriculum guide] pretty well, but what I found was that I, I'm one of these persons who doesn't like to have everything mapped out. Because what happens is I start asserting too much outside control. I look at my day-to-day outline and I see that, 'Oh Man, we might be falling behind, let's hurry up and do that.'"

Nick's statements on teachers' attributes and teacher identity can explain in part some of his resistance to scholarly analysis of teaching theory and pedagogy and pedagogical modeling. Nick's sense of the attributes of a good teacher underscore his own sense of teaching strengths and areas that need change. Nick tended to describe a writing teacher by affective and performance strengths—as someone who was tireless, enthusiastic, gregarious, sensitive to student needs, informal, facilitating, counseling, and comradely. A teacher could be a guru-guide, a performer, the Jim McMahon of the writing classroom, a magician, jocular, upbeat, and a shrewd judge of his classroom audience: students. Relatively undiscussed was the teacher's cognitive development—the need to know the field, to assimilate and integrate theory with practice, to be experienced, and so on. Not unexpectedly, though, all of the ready adjectives or personas a teacher could have still didn't lend certainty to classroom teaching. Nick related that "just two weeks ago I thought I had a solid grip on my role as a writing teacher, but now I'm not so sure."

Nick and Performance

As he pondered these issues, one major worry surfaced: Nick's self-reported tendency towards performance which included talking a lot and being at center stage in the classroom. Nick first abandoned his allegiance to his performance stance, saying he had to change. But slowly, during the course of the Teaching Basic Writing seminar, in learning log entries, he reconsidered his favorite model of teacher-as-performer and questioned whether it couldn't still be a viable model for him. "Perhaps I'm overreacting," he said. "Perhaps I've fallen victim to the old either-or fallacy." Nick continued to explore ways he could take new material and "make it mine," and at times he seemed to equivocate. "I know that I have to let my students take charge, but is there anything wrong with my being their guru-guide?" By the time he completed his fall 1987 class, he could say, "I think what I do is, I try to take something and have it suit my personality," and "I know I can't change my personality." At the same time he noted that his natural talent for producing lively, entertaining material for his audience was risky. "At times students forget the reason for that kind of approach. The reason for the humor. They tend at times to go to class and enjoy themselves rather than to learn."

Nick's focus on the teacher-as-performer was not surprising, for two reasons. First, he had in recent years started teaching speech classes and coaching the college debating team, so he had a heightened awareness of the effectiveness of oral presentation of material. Second, he had a great appreciation for Tom Bridges's teaching style. He characterized Bridges as a like-minded teacher, one who used humor and entertained his classes, and as a highly successful instructor. ("Last night I was inspired; after today's class, that inspiration is turning into commitment. Now is that a sign of effective instruction [on Bridges's part] or what?") And Nick appeared to model some of his activities and justify some of his own predispositions by relating his close affinity to Bridges, who Nick saw as an ideal model teacher. Nick pointed out that Bridges effectively did the same things in the same ways as Nick did them, or intended to do them. "I'm convinced that even though Tom himself is sold on the process instruction, there's no doubt about that, I think that we're all willing to admit that he is one of those teachers who likes teacher-centered performance as long as it doesn't interfere with the process. And I'm sure that I will figure out ways in which I can—I can make myself fulfil myself as an actor and at the same time make sure that my students are getting as much from—the course."

Nick also believed he saw a Bridges that few other participants saw—one who was fond of teacher-centered performance, one who could look at Nick and know who and what Nick was, one who could be seen or who saw himself as "a writing savior," one who was "uncannily" similar to Nick in pedagogical matters, one who was witty in a way unappreciated by classmates, one who was best savored during instances of teacher lecture because he was an excellent speaker ("Wasn't Friday's class one of the best of the sessions—if not the best—because of our seeing Bridges do what he does best—talk to us?"), and one who used conferences in a way identical to the way Nick used conferences ("I'm using conferencing, and, like Tom, I think I have a tendency to talk too much—but my students don't seem to mind").

All of these may be true attributes of both Tom Bridges and Nick, for other participants mentioned Tom's humor, energy, and charismatic classroom personality. What also appears true is that Nick, was to a certain extent, validating his writing classroom model by developing his own teaching identity based on a model teacher, although he appeared aware of possible dangers of such a model when he stated that he wasn't going to "become a Bridges-ite." Keeping these developments in mind, it is now useful to look at Nick's class, fall 1987.

Nick's Home Institution and Writing Class

Nick teaches at a community college that serves a western Pennsylvania county and offers two-year degrees and certificates. Students can enroll full time or part time, and a large number of evening classes are offered. In discussing his class enrollment, Nick sometimes differentiated between "young" students, those just out of high school, and "older" students, who often seemed more committed to interacting in class and producing writing.

The course which was studied in this research project was ENG 161, College Writing, the college preparatory freshman English course. The catalog description of ENG 161 follows.

ENG 161 covers the fundamentals of college writing including the paragraph, the expository essay patterns and the argumentative essay. Emphasis is placed on organizing materials coherently, writing concisely and clearly and adapting one's writing to a particular audience. This course is also concerned with self-editing, mechanics, grammar, spelling improvement and vocabulary development. ENG 161 thus provides the foundation needed for students to concentrate later on effectively producing a range of writing from technical reports, to business communications, to research and critical papers.

Prerequisite: ENG 100 or satisfactory score on English placement test.

Nick's "Course Outline" lists no mandated course goals. His course objectives come directly from the curriculum guide and rationale that he prepared for Teaching Basic Writing. This list of course goals immediately introduced the vocabulary of the writing workshop and shifted the emphasis from product, as seen in the catalog description—concern with surface level correctness—to process: "The student will develop an improved attitude toward writing," or "The student will develop writing fluency."

Students were told they would "submit drafts of papers on at least 5 mutually agreed upon topics." After conferencing with the teacher, students had the option of revising and resubmitting the paper for "folder" evaluation and grade or writing another draft that they shared with the peer-response group *before* presenting it to the teacher for evaluation.

Class Assignments

Nick began the semester by relying on his curriculum guide and rationale, developed for Teaching Basic Writing, although he mentioned moving away from it as the semester progressed. Tom Bridges responded favorably to Nick's curriculum guide, primarily making a few anti-instructional scaffolding comments in the margins. Bridges felt that Nick had extended the guide in interesting ways by including rationales for using "speaking" or "talk" in the classroom, and Nick also included an objective intended to allow students to "make sense of his or her world"—by which Nick meant that students would learn to move from inner to outer worlds or from writer-based to reader-based prose considerations.

Nick made the fullest possible use of the Bridges assignment generator. Throughout the semester, students wrote on topics of their choice and turned the papers in when they felt ready. Each set of papers that I collected contained a diversity in student subject matter. Students were responsible for producing a minimum of five essays and a journal.

In-class work often focused on student journals. Weekly, students wrote in class on topics developed or guided by Nick and then shared responses aloud. Every student either read or, more often, summarized what he or she had written. Other in-class work included both previously developed class activities (used by Nick in earlier semesters) for discussing writing voice and style by considering sample essays, and new activities that Nick had participated in himself in doctoral classes, such as a note card invention exercise.

Writing Evaluation

Nick introduced the assignment generator to the class early in the semester and used it as a springboard for class discussion. Students drafted papers at their own speed and then shared them with a peer response group, usually on Fridays. Students shared papers with the teacher in conference, but usually outside of class. Due to heavy departmental demands on Nick's time, by the end of his fall writing class, out-of-class conference time had shrunk—from an original "20 minutes per student times twenty students" to "about an hour of conferencing a week."

Nick relied on conferencing in a new way during this semester, as a time to verbally evaluate student writing. He no longer took papers home on the weekend for marathon grading sessions, and he found himself, at first, doing most of his paper evaluation on campus. At midsemester, students submitted their best piece for a conference evaluation. For this conference, Nick did take the pieces home and wrote comments intended to focus on major order concerns: organization, development, voice, and so on.

A sample of early writings show his students writing about a variety of topics. A sampling of such papers included "Professional Manicure Procedure," "A Dream," a selection of three poems, a fairy tale, an essay about living on a farm, and an essay about how the writer spent her Christmas.

On the draft of the Christmas essay, Nick commented in the margins as he read, and he ended with a summative paragraph. Marginal comments consisted exclusively of questions. "Does this comment really clarify this point?" "Have you captured the joyousness of this occasion?" "But should you leave such a feast to my imagination?" "What do you all do for such a long time?" "What kinds of things? Does the food here differ from the evening feast?" "What are some of the unique yet traditional Serbian treats?" All of these comments asked for clarification, addition, detail. The final summary comment read: "Danielle—you've given me some interesting clues about how your Christmas differs from mine, but I still have a ton of questions—when do you exchange presents? or do you? do you have a Santa Claus? How do Serbian kids deal with their traditional Christmas friends? Are there any special legends you could share? I remember you saying you thought this topic might be boring—but it seems to me that there's some potentially interesting stuff here."

These summary comments asked a number of additional questions and referred back to an earlier discussion about the paper. Nick never marked on the text or addressed usage concerns in writing. On other papers, questions and exclamations of heartfelt reader response ("Whew! you seem to be hitting me with too many rapid-fire bits of info") are the major response patterns.

The second set of papers contained responses that were remarkably similar to those on the first set. Although generated much later in the semester, papers still covered a diverse range of topics and Nick used the same response system. However, responses to one unsatisfactory student-generated assignment reflected some of the problems involved for any teacher using the assignment generator. The paper consisted of a short cover letter to a friend concerning a local cookbook and a second page with three short recipes intended for that cookbook. Nick's summary comment reads: "Good personal touches [response to statements about mixing batter, such as: 'Beat like heck'] but as we've already discussed, Julia, I'm not really certain about how to judge this as a piece of writing. I would imagine that you've covered all the bases well, but I was hoping that the papers that you submit would require more 'creative' writing of you, if you know what I mean. But thanks for taking advantage of the opportunity to write those pieces that you truly want to do. It's just that recipes don't seem to demand enough writing, per se."

With this paper, we see Nick as evaluator trying to balance the roles of coach and sensitive reader with his roles as evaluator and teacher responsible to the institutional demands for freshman writing competency. He appeared to remain committed to his goal of developing student choice of topics. At the same time, it was not clear from these samples if any ordering process helped students achieve Nick's curriculum guide goal—to move from inner to outer worlds, in a developmental sequence.

A Typical Week

Nick divided almost three-quarters of his class time between teacher-led whole group discussion (25 percent); small group activities (25 percent), during which he more often talked with a single group (20 percent of small group time) than conducted in-class conferences (5 percent of small group time); and student in-class writing (20 percent). Another 15 percent of class time was devoted to teacher lecture, which Nick characterized as students "sitting around the campfire" and looking to the teacher as group leader. Nick believed the whole group discussion dynamic was different, with students voluntarily taking part in the talk and the class focus shifting from speaker to speaker. The miscellaneous category (10 percent) included class give-and-take, question asking, assignment explication, general directions, etc. Nick didn't give out a semester-long schedule, so he tended to give the next week's overview during the Friday meeting of his class, which met Monday, Wednesday, and Friday.

Students in Nick's class sat in lightweight plastic chairs that were equipped with writing arms. For the first two and one-half hours (two and one-half days) of video taping, students remained in rows. During the final one-half hour on the third day of class, when they formed peer groups, they moved their chairs around. The class tape confirmed Nick's estimate of class time for modes and activities in general. In teacher-led discussion of paper evaluation criteria, Nick would prompt the class and record volunteers' answers on the board. Then Nick signaled a journal writing period. At the end of the writing period, a few students' answers were shared, and these were fielded by Nick who made jokes and shared his own impressions. During this and other journal response times, Nick responded from the front of class with stories (of times similar experiences happened to him) or jokes intended to encourage ready response from the students.

When Nick asked the class to work in groups on papers they were writing, he returned some papers as groups worked and joked with different group members, sometimes from a stationary location at the front, sometimes as he joined the groups. In some groups, members appeared to be prepared and read papers aloud to each other. At least one large group floundered a bit; no single student seemed to be prepared until quite near the end of the period, when one woman read her paper.

In an interview conducted after the video taping, Nick pointed out that the amount of time spent on journal writing and sharing (thirty minutes on the first day, Monday; forty-five minutes on the second day, Wednesday) was a bit high that week, particularly in the time it took for each student to share his or her writing ideas. He also confirmed that the humor observed in his class was important to him as a way to connect with students as human beings and interest them in coming to class.

For Nick's class, outside activities shifted in focus as the semester progressed. During the first half of the semester, more than three-fourths of his ten hours a week outside the classroom (for this class) were spent in student/teacher conferences and only brief periods were spent in paper evaluation, primarily the type of comments listed above. Class preparation was equally brief throughout the semester. Nick explained, "I found the burden [of class preparation] really was lifted from me because as soon as I came up with an activity or an idea I would simply think about how to make it work. So It wasn't actual preparing where you could say, 'Look at Nick, he's preparing.'" By the end of the semester, class preparation and evaluation time continued to occupy about one to two hours per week, but out of class conferencing had dropped dramatically because Nick had become involved in departmental work that drastically reduced available professional time and drained his affective energies. Conferences for this class dropped from eight out of ten hours to one out of two hours each week. Nick felt this reduction was the major flaw in his semester. Also dropped due to time constraints were the editorial board (used once during the first half of the semester) and publishing (planned but never instituted). Nick became so busy he simply forgot these activities.

The following activities or techniques were important instructional focuses in the Teaching Basic Writing seminar:

- Bridges assignment generator
  (or encouraging student-generated writing topics)
- peer writing groups
- sentence combining
- editorial board
- student journals or learning logs
- in-class student/teacher conferences
- teacher sharing his/her own writing
- publishing student writing
- formal measures to evaluate the writing classroom

Use of these activities and techniques was seen as supportive of the whole language, writing workshop classroom as developed in that seminar.

Nick started out the semester with the *assignment generator* as the organizing principle for his course. He felt it was successful, but he planned to set a few deadlines the next time he used it, providing for folder evaluation during the fifth, tenth, and final weeks of the semester. Generally, students used the generator with few problems, yet Nick felt a certain number of students continued to generate just "school" topics and some procrastinated excessively.

Peer work was instituted as a regular part of the paper review process. Students were given training documents and were expected to read aloud early drafts of work with peers before conferencing with the teacher. Group membership remained stable throughout the semester because of Nick's own experience in the TBW seminar learning log group. The experience taught him that group members need to develop a sense of trust in order to share freely about personal matters. One student told him she would have liked to change groups in order to receive new input, and another told him she liked having the groups retain the original membership because that allowed her to share very personal work. Since he valued personal investment highly in writing, Nick felt he would continue with semester-long group membership.

Nick had students evaluate the classroom and group work in written responses. Most were positive about the class. Five people directly requested more group work, and this seemed to reflect a positive class attitude and perhaps a need for even more time in this valuable teaching mode.

In-class conferencing was used much less often than teacher visits to groups. Nick said he expected that pattern to remain stable. "I know that Tom recommended that the teacher sometimes walks away from the groups and that anyone who wants to see the teacher come up to the front. But I find that I think things go pretty well for me when I wander around and sit down with each group and give a kind of a small group conference so I'm going to have to think about that." When he did hold in-class conferences, Nick indicated he may have focused on technical rather than content level concerns during these second draft, brief interactions.

Nick convened an *editorial board* once but forgot to use it near the end of the semester. His lack of engagement, he believed, stemmed partly from the fact that students were working on pieces at their own pace, and there were few occasions requiring such a board. It was necessary, really, only for midsemester and end-of-semester folder evaluations. He said that he forgot class publication entirely. Because he was "philosophically opposed" to *sentence combining*, viewing it as little different than direct grammar instruction (which he also did not use), no direct instructional use of sentence combining took place.

Journals were important in this class and Nick intended to keep them as a central activity in future classes. Students wrote in their journals under Nick's direction nearly every class period. They shared their writings, and these writings were a large factor in the grades of some students.

Early in the semester, Nick *shared a sample of his writing.* He asked students to critique a letter he had written to a former friend, one who was no longer responding to letters. This was a unique experience for Nick. He had never previously felt willing to let his students critique him. As the letter was quite personal in content and informal in tone, he felt it performed an important function, showing him as human and as a peer to his students. Later in the semester, Nick spoke to his students about doctoral program writing projects but did not share them.

No methods for regularly *publishing student writing* were instituted in this classroom, although Nick had mused during summer interviews over possible access to the student newspaper. In his curriculum guide, Nick mentioned many *classroom evaluation measures* he might use. Like many teachers, though, he did not complete any formal evaluation procedure. He scored early Writing Apprehension surveys and circulated a questionnaire, mentioned above, asking for student response to the class and to group work, but he did not complete end-of-class evaluation measures. He said of himself, "I'm not one of these who gets turned on to objective data. I appreciate that you [the researcher] are doing an ethnography rather than setting up a particular test. Because I think when you start measuring things you start losing, like human beings."

This belief that the classroom evaluation measures were artificial, along with the reality of time constraints, kept Nick from formal methods of evaluating his writing classroom. Although he did not institute formal measures, he still felt the class had been highly successful. "I'm excited about the results [of the semester] because I think I made a difference. But that's something that I don't know is measurable. But I know I made a difference."

Students in Nick's writing class generally confirmed this class picture. Some slight variations in students' and teacher's perceptions about the frequency of activities can be explained. Students seemed to view the samples of essays that Nick brought in to illuminate stylistic concerns as traditional classroom writing models. They also seemed to believe that teacher-led collaborative brainstorming was not as representative of writing a piece together as Nick did. In most other areas, students and teacher were in considerable agreement about class activities.

This classroom, from both teacher and student perspectives, encompassed a number of the techniques and activities proposed in the Teaching Basic Writing seminar, but the proportions evidenced Nick's personal interests and were quite different from those found in the conference-based workshop approach of Peg's writing classroom. Nick's class relied on teacher interaction with groups—what

Nick called group conferences—and teacher-led discussions with Nick orchestrating, coaching, and fielding student sharing of journals, and so on; Nick was often most active at the center of his classroom. Also, several of the activities reviewed here, particularly the editorial board and out of class conferencing disappeared or were limited in scope later in the semester.

Discussion

For Nick, as for any writing teacher, the development of a teaching identity or persona was a complex undertaking. Nick's movement through the doctoral program and back to his teaching classroom illuminated this complexity.

It was clear that teachers entered the doctoral program in rhetoric with teaching pasts that affected how they assimilated new materials. As doctoral students, they were expected to demonstrate a range of new knowledge in the field of composition studies while they integrated themselves into a community that shared a common "model of knowing," the graduate program ideology. Berkenkotter, Huckin, and Ackerman (1988) describe this process. "Graduate students are initiated into the research community through the reading and writing they do, through instruction in research methodology, and through interaction with faculty and with their peers" (p. 12).

Just as past experiences helped participants assimilate new materials, past experiences slowed down the assimilation or change process, as in the study by Berkenkotter, et al., where the doctoral level writer they observed had some difficulty moving from writing informally in his own voice to writing formally, in the accepted manner of the discipline. His "multi-register fluency was impeded by his political and practical preferences for expressive discourse which preceded his graduate studies and his relative ignorance of a complex and far-reaching corpus of scholarship" (p. 38) (see Schilb [1988] for a critique of the implicit assumption in this article that such student accommodation is desired and desirable).

In much the same way, Nick made efforts to maintain his personal writing voice even while pointing out his need to write to doctoral program professors as authority figures. Asserting a personal voice in his writing was an indication of one of Nick's largest concerns, that of developing a clear identity both as a doctoral student and as a teacher of writing.

Developing a teaching identity is a complex process, in part because teachers rarely gather together. Like Peg in the previous case study, teachers can find themselves cut off from professional support; or like Nick, commuter students can find they stand back from a peer network that they view with suspicion due to a self-perceived (or real) outsider status. Russell (1988) explains teachers' isolation this way.

> Unfortunately, opportunities to learn from other teachers, to be part of a conscious teaching tradition, are rare in the modern academic community. Teaching is one of the performing arts, situational, immediate, improvisational yet planned. And despite the alienation of the modern university, teachers ultimately learn from one another, face to face, as do all performing artists. Without a strong sense of a teaching community, traditions develop more slowly and less consciously than in plastic or literary arts, where models are visible and permanent (as the long dominance of "current-traditional" pedagogy illustrates) but they do develop, for better or worse. (p. 443)

Teachers in a doctoral program may develop identities by slow initiation into the research community through their writing and course work and by a complex process of doubting and believing as they sift through theory and methodology. This process was indicated in Nick's case by his attempt to find right or wrong ways (consistency in eclecticism) and by his efforts to model himself on the teachers who taught him. In the Teaching Basic Writing seminar, Nick developed strong identification with Tom Bridges as a model teacher.

As doctoral participants encountered new materials in Teaching Basic Writing, they assimilated these materials through the classroom discussions and lectures, their own writing of learning logs and sharing in learning log groups, and their peer interactions. As participants in a doctoral program, they were often asked to evaluate research and theory, to take an essentially doubting position, disconfirming materials when necessary. As participants in Teaching Basic Writing, they were asked to take a believing stance toward the organized materials in Tom Bridges's seminar—a stance that would lead them to the development of a whole language, writing workshop classroom.

Elbow (1986b) posits methodological doubting and believing as essential learning activities. He claims that we more often doubt than believe, needing only one disconfirmation to abandon an assertion. Proof of the nonexistence of a disconfirming instance, however, is difficult (if not impossible) to provide. Elbow claims that doubt too often caters to "our natural impulse to protect and retain the views we already hold" (p. 263).

Nick, though often involved with both doubting and believing, in his sincere effort to find a philosophical base or a way, most often dealt with doubt in his study of and reactions to class materials, even going so far as to describe himself as resident "heretic." What seemed missing from his search was the element of a consistent methodology that would allow him to develop new beliefs *intellectually as well as affectively.* As he sorted through theory, for instance that of sentence combining, Nick responded to research reports with his personal, long-term dislike of research and justified his abandonment of sentence combining due to an affective response. For Nick, sentence combining *felt* too much like direct grammar instruction. He did not appear to have developed a way to organize doubt and belief. Elbow (1986b) describes organized doubting and believing as leading to "artificial, systematic, and disciplined uses of the mind. As methods, they help us see what we would miss if we only use our minds naturally or spontaneously" (p. 258).

Brooke, in two discussions of writing, the teaching of writing, and identity formation (1987, 1988), offers information about identity formation for writers that rings true for teachers-as-learners, also. Brooke posits the need for students in classrooms to participate in "underlife," where "actors in an institution develop behaviors which assert an identity different from the one assigned them" (1987, p. 143). For instance, Nick refused the doctoral persona of a writer who will write "publishable quality" papers. He considered and reconsidered his teacher-as-performer identity, first conceding to TBW seminar pressure to work at the edges of the classroom, and then, gradually, finding reasons to reassert his previous performance-based identity.

As described by Brooke (1987), identity assertion is a natural result of learning. "No one but the complete fanatic completely associates herself with only one role—instead, the self is formed in the distance one takes from the roles one is assigned. In such an analysis, activities which aren't on task become as important as activities which are, for besides the task itself there is also always the formation of identity" (p. 144).

Nick's concern with his classroom identity confirms the importance of this aspect of learning in the Teaching Basic Writing seminar, as do the observations of Perl and Wilson (1986).

> We realized that just as there is no one way to write so there is no one way to teach writing. Rather, how teachers teach writing, or probably anything else for that matter, is a function of who they are, what matters to them, what they bring with them into the classroom, and whom they meet there. How they go about their work can be affected in certain important ways by conditions in the school, in the community, in the culture at large, but what affects teaching most deeply and dramatically are the themes, the interests, and the deeply felt concerns that affect and give shape to teachers' lives. (p. 248)

During the pedagogy seminar, Nick mentioned influences that would be important for his fall 1987 writing classroom: his love of humor in the classroom, his love of performance, his current involvement in teaching speech, and his appreciation of Tom Bridges as a model teacher who, for Nick, embodied some of his own (Nick's) teaching attributes. Russell (1988) argues that teachers learn to be teachers through such modeling, although two contradictory views of teacher-as-model exist.

> As artists, writing teachers perfect their craft through theoretical principles, models for imitation, and practice guided by a master (a *magister*, a teacher). In each of these, traditions are central. But modern writing teaching, like modern writing, has been shackled by two competing views, both of which distrust tradition and create alienation: a mechanical scientism, ahistorical in its incessant pursuit of progress, and a romanticism which locates teaching (and writing) in the native genius of the individual, independent of historical and social processes. (p. 437)

Nick is clearly of the latter view, ascribing to an individualistic teaching romanticism which leads him to judge his class success affectively, by the fact of his "having made a difference." He appeared not yet to have merged those views, as Russell (1987) advocates, just as he had not yet developed his ability to develop methodological doubting and believing. He was, therefore, somewhat under the sway of what Russell calls "the agony of influence" (p. 438). Nick found, in his interpretation of Tom Bridges's teaching, confirmation for his own "identity theme." Holland (1980) explains the identity theme. "This primary identity stands as an invariant which provides all the later transformations of the individual, as he develops, with an unchanging inner form or core of continuity" (p. 121).

And for Holland, the "personality" or "character" is developed from "the millions of ego choices that constitute the visible human before me" (p. 121). Nick's consideration of just how performance-oriented and just how humorous he could be in the classroom, and still create a truly student-centered classroom as he wished to, showed the process of ego choices in action. And, at the end of his set of interviews, Nick reached much the same conclusion as did Holland—that he "can't change his personality."

Perl and Wilson (1986) found that one of their case study teachers who had a dominant personality encountered student resistance in his classroom. A performance oriented teacher, Ross, "as much as any other teacher in the study took the principles of the writing process approach to heart" (p. 148), yet Ross still had difficulties during the semester he was observed by Perl. Perl found him overly dominant in the classroom. In a subsequent year, this teacher had a more successful time teaching, and although he learned how to stand back, somewhat, he still could not alter his classroom personality drastically without teaching against himself. In a similar way, Nick realized that the collaborative classroom he was considering during the TBW seminar was going to require that he mute his classroom persona in some ways that might be impossible.

The fall 1987 classroom that Nick conducted was satisfying, both to himself and to his students. At the beginning, Nick instituted many changes—more peer work than formerly, a lot of supportive conferencing, and so on. As the semester wore on, outside pressures eroded both his classroom model and his enthusiasm. He found less time for some of his activities, and he still projected (and finally justified to himself) a relatively high teacher profile in the classroom. The fall classroom Nick developed was not the same classroom he discussed as an "ideal" in Teaching Basic Writing, nor was it quite the same classroom predicted in Nick's curriculum guide. For instance, like many other teachers, Nick left out the formalized classroom evaluation measures—an important part of Bridges's classroom model and of Nick's curriculum guide. At this point, Nick was no longer emulating Bridges completely but was developing a practical version of the "ideal" writing classroom and the "ideal" writing teacher.

Brooke (1988) points out that modeling is an uncertain process. "The teacher, no matter how exciting a model she presents, just isn't in control of the identity the student will develop. Students are not as tractable as that—the identities they negotiate in any class are the result, to a large extent, of the identities they already have" (p. 38). The identity Nick forged was, perhaps, similar to that he perceived as Bridges's in the graduate seminar, but it was less similar to the identity Bridges was advocating for the collaborative classroom. In such a classroom, Perl and Wilson explained, teachers have to learn to "'get out of the way'" (1986, p. 256). Getting out of the way seems to indicate a model that is less performance-based, one that places the teacher supportively at the side rather than at the center of the classroom. And getting out of the way as a collaborative technique is illuminated in Elbow's methodological believing stance referred to above. Elbow (1986b) believes that gender influences doubting and believing. He lists many attributes of each stance, as summarized here.

1. doubting = resisting authority, disengagement from action or holding back, tentativeness and conditionality, trial by fire and "invites behaviors which our culture associates with masculinity: refusing, saying No, pushing away, competing, being aggressive . . . interrupting and making noise."

2. believing = acquiescence, action, total conviction or certainty of feeling, consensus and participation and "invites behaviors associated with femininity: accepting, saying Yes, being compliant, listening, absorbing, and swallowing . . . being mute or silent." (pp. 264–265)

And Emig (1983) thinks that believing behaviors may be more easily implemented for women than for men.

> I think this is the first time I'm going to talk about men and women as teachers. In my experience, and it may or may not be representative, men teach as a revelation, as an expression of ego. Ego teaching has no use at all if you're trying to teach writing and rhetoric, from any other than a historical aspect. The only ego that should be of interest in the teaching of writing is the ego of the writer, which means that the ego of the teacher has somehow to stand aside. In my experience, most men aren't capable of getting out of the way. I think that's the reason there is very poor teaching of writing. I think women, in my experience, are often very, very good teachers of writing because they're willing to put their ego aside. It seems to me the purpose of the teacher is to enhance the writing process so the student can find something to say. By the way, it's not self-abnegation. To me, it's extremely arrogant to decide not to participate. (pp. 132–133)

Nick's search for a way to conflate his strongly performance-based teaching identity with a strongly collaborative (and hence back-grounded) teaching identity, illustrated a difficulty all teachers have—understanding that feminine behaviors are not ego-less or self-abnegating, in spite of a culture that tells us such behaviors are less than desirable. Given the female dominance of the composition teaching profession, such gender-based concerns may become of primary importance for teachers beginning to incorporate new teaching practices into their writing classrooms and their teaching identities (Flynn, 1988).

Nick desired changes. He wanted to step back and develop a less teacher-centered classroom. His frequent uses of quest images and his many references to religious conversion underscored this strong desire to change his teaching practices and his identity so he wouldn't have to call himself a "charlatan." Nick may have under-estimated the complexity of the task he set himself and the necessity to develop a stronger base for change than enthusiasm, tirelessness, and so on—teaching traits that ran out for him during a difficult semester. In this, he was similar to Peg in a previous case study (and perhaps to many other teachers), in that Nick relied on his own affective state for the strength of his classroom.

In terms of Crocker, Fiske, & Taylor's 1984 study of models of schema building, bookkeeping, conversion, and subtyping, Nick verbally embodied conversion through his choice of metaphorical comparisons and remarks (what I call "verbal conversion"), but he did not seem to undergo the type of sudden change in practice the conversion model points to. Instead, like Susan in a previous case study, he appeared to sub-type material, even as he described himself as changing, and he stored new information that he might or might not activate.

This analysis of the complex process of change that Nick experienced needs to take into account the real and practical occurrences of his writing classroom: both the students and Nick were comfortable. The students had lowered writing apprehension and wrote exclusively on topics of their own choosing. These activities supported Nick's overall class goals of giving more power to students and increasing, foremost, their writing fluency and ownership of text. As Nick explained his own change in the last interview, "This was really the first version of the new me. It's going to take some more revising."

6

Julia, a College Level Teacher of Writing: Transforming Kids and Students into Writers and Peers

I have just really felt that for the first time I have treated these students as human beings.

—Interview with Julia, fall 1987

JULIA ENROLLED IN THE GATTON UNIVERSITY DOCTORAL PROgram because she was interested in continuing her education and because of the urging of a colleague at her institution who had completed a similar degree in the doctoral program several years earlier. After teaching for eight years at the high school level, Julia worked as a school administrator for five years before taking up college teaching. At the time of this research, she had taught for three years at her current institution, a small campus of a major southeastern university.

Before enrolling in the doctoral program, Julia was a relatively self-taught writing teacher. She explained, "The idea of becoming a *writing* teacher came to me long after I had been teaching *English*." She had no formal training courses or workshops in teaching writing and modeled her teaching style on that of her own high school English teacher whom she termed a "grammarian and traditionalist."

Julia wrote frequently and in many modes and published income-producing journalism in local papers. She explained her relationship to writing as a positive one. "I write daily which shows my love for it. I don't know if my writing is all that good—it says what I want and need to say."

However, at the beginning of the Gatton University doctoral program, Julia registered mixed feelings about herself as a composition teacher, terming herself as self-taught, focused on grammar, and as someone who changed, "solely dependent on my mood." She did not appear to have strong leanings in any pedagogical direction (neither desiring to begin with a clean slate, as in Peg's case study, nor terming herself already heavily involved in process paradigm change, as in Nick's case study). Like Rosalyn in a previous case study, Julia was very involved with students. "My philosophy has been to help as many students as I can to improve their writing skills. I see improvement, by and large, in many." She had a quiet expectation that she would grow through her participation in the doctoral program, but she appeared relatively open about what she expected. Julia saw classroom change as teacher instigated. She said she changed from semester to semester, mainly in order to "vary" the class "for my benefit, I suppose, in all honesty." When, twice, she rather musingly wondered if she wouldn't perhaps learn some new methods through her doctoral program participation, Julia appeared unsure of what she would encounter, but she also was not particularly nervous about the future.

Julia's pedagogical concerns at the beginning of doctoral course work were not extensive, although her view of herself as a structured, possibly traditional, grammar-focused teacher came out clearly. Her strengths as a teacher of writing dealt with other areas. She felt able to stimulate students to think about topics, to help them to organize their thoughts, and to help them realize that they had something to say—although she felt the last was difficult to accomplish.

Before participating in the pedagogy seminar, Julia's most used teaching techniques consisted of small group writing, free writing, sharing paragraph writing or journals, and entertaining students' questions about writing—essentially invention and discussion techniques.

Julia and the Doctoral Program

Julia came to the doctoral program for the usual mixed set of reasons. Getting a Ph.D. would help her maintain or improve her current teaching position, a nontenure track instructorship. Additionally, she had been encouraged to attend by a program graduate who told her she would fit into the Gatton University program well. Finally, Julia had always expected to go on with her education, to work toward a Ph.D. Now that she was in her early forties, the time for doing so was slipping away, and she realized that she had better begin.

Julia was a doctoral program participant who registered a great deal of surprise at the rigor of the Gatton University Ph.D. degree in English/Rhetoric and Linguistics. She felt overwhelmed by the work demands during her first week of summer session study and almost resented the colleague who had assured her she would fit in so easily. Julia said, "You know, I wrote her and said, I wish you'd *told* me [how hard it would be]." Julia said that she might have left the graduate program if she hadn't told all her friends what she was doing and if leaving wouldn't have represented such a loss of face.

These feelings changed as Julia successfully completed the first, five-week, summer session, taking classes in second language acquisition and linguistics. Her sense of staying mostly to save face converted to an enthusiasm for what she was learning. "I want to learn about this, all of this." She found she had real questions about students who were less successful than she would have liked them to be in her classes, and she hoped the Teaching Basic Writing seminar would lead her to a deeper understanding of her writing classroom.

Julia also responded positively to Tom Bridges, the training seminar instructor. As the seminar began, she viewed him as a model teacher, and, like Nick in a previous case study, described some of Bridges's teaching attributes as those attributes she felt were her own strong points.

Julia: Now I think he is, Bridges, is, probably he is good, great, teaching this course because he is such a good model, I think, of what a good teacher is.

Researcher: Can you give me a quick definition of what that is? What you're seeing, what that model is?
Julia: Well. Uh, the energy. His energy. Because I, you know in teaching I think that the energy I have for whatever subject it is whether it's a short story or whether its an essay but if I can just kind of transfer my energy to my students————

Julia had a self-declared history of teacher modeling. Her own first model was her high school English teacher with whom she still kept in contact. This teacher came and visited Julia during the doctoral program summer sessions. At the same time, Julia mentored a former high school student of her own who was herself teaching high school. Julia received teaching advice and shared teaching triumphs with both these women, producing a unique sharing chain through three generations of high school English teachers.

For Julia, then, teacher modeling was natural but not dominant; she acknowledged influences in a few anecdotes. Unlike Nick in a previous case study, although Julia saw some parallels between her own teaching style and that of Tom Bridges, she did not mention him as a model very often, spending more time reflecting on her own development and her teaching past.

Julia's Concerns

While enrolled in the Teaching Basic Writing seminar at Gatton University, Julia often volunteered anecdotes of her previously prescriptive teaching practices. This allegiance to a current-traditional, teacher-centered teaching paradigm shifted by the end of the pedagogy seminar. During the Teaching Basic Writing seminar she read research in composing, kept a learning log and participated in a learning log group, entered into class discussions, and generally reconsidered her teaching philosophy in order to write her final project—a curriculum guide and rationale that instituted what was, for her, a new teaching model: the whole language, writing workshop where the teacher is coach, supporting students' development. Through these activities, Julia moved from viewing herself as a grammarian (as she began the training seminar) to viewing herself as not-a-grammarian (at the end of the fall 1987 freshman writing class she taught at her home institution). At the same time, Julia moved from seeing herself as someone who didn't change, or might not change, to someone who had changed, and had possibly always changed a bit more than she had realized. Finally, her changed perceptions of herself and her altered teaching methods led her to a new view of her students. She moved from an early hierarchical structure where she saw students as "kids" and herself as "teacher" to a more equivalent structure where she saw students and herself as "adults," "peers," and "writers." This interrelated process of change in pedagogy *and* affect can be traced.

Julia as a Grammarian

Julia began her teaching career by modeling on her high school teacher who taught prescriptively. She never thought to question the model by which she was learning, just as she didn't question it in her own early teaching. That is, she followed the rules of "what I perceived to be my job as an English teacher," in spite of the fact that for some students this method didn't work at all. She knew that "some kids you can correct all day until you're blue in the [face]—for ten years, and they'll never pay attention to anything." Because Julia herself learned well through a traditional approach, she may have assumed that any flaw in the method resided in the students, in their (in)ability or (un)willingness to work, rather than in the fact that for some students the traditional approach may have been unsuitable.

So strong was Julia's expectation that a writing teacher was mainly a grammarian, a paper-marking evaluator, she dreaded returning to her fall 1987 college writing class, knowing she would be in for endless grading sessions due to a heavy classload. "I, I'm not looking forward to getting back to the semester to school because I spend all my time grading papers. I mean I grade papers until two o'clock in the morning. I'm, I'm going to do that a little bit differently this fall." Even in this expectation, though, she voiced a desire to change that burdensome model, and near the end of the Teaching Basic Writing seminar, she became convinced that she had to introduce a more student-centered classroom model, one that would challenge her evaluation procedures:

Researcher: Tell me three things you now believe about teaching writing?

Julia: That it has to be student-centered. That it has to be student-owned and I cannot, *look*—this is the most important thing I've learned—that I cannot take it and just [sound of shaking papers], crumble it up like I normally do. And when I say crumble it up [student's paper] I mean, you know, write all over it.

And, in her TBW seminar learning log, Julia admitted she was (and had been) aware of the research showing the relative ineffectiveness of direct grammar instruction. For Julia, as for other teachers, knowing that direct grammar instruction was ineffective and putting that knowledge to use in the classroom were two different situations. Never a fan of theory, Julia said, "I look at this class [TBW seminar], Wendy, as a real practical tool and sometimes, sometimes it's—it sort of goes over my head a little bit with analysis and theory."

Like other practicing teachers, Julia struggled to understand how the ideal model of the whole language, writing workshop would actually function when she returned to teaching. Should she give up her charts that listed the errors students made on papers? Should she keep marking on papers in red ink? Should she questions whether revised papers were the students' own work? How should she assign grades for revised work, and so on?

Even in her pedagogy seminar learning log, Julia was beginning to reconceptualize herself, terming herself less a grammarian as she moved towards allegiance to the whole language, writing workshop classroom model advocated by Tom Bridges. During the seminar, Julia would raise her hand and jokingly "confess" to formerly rigid or grammar-oriented evaluation methods. As she studied and learned, she was able to see herself as more liberal than one of the writers on grading methods (Larson, 1986). Writing in her log, she asked, "Who's this writer [Larson] kidding? There are some things in this article that even I, the old semi-prescriptive, teacher wouldn't do!"

Julia's first step in her reconceptualization process seemed to be to see herself as *previously* prescriptive. Then, during her fall 1987 writing class, she described herself as holding back on directive evaluation and intentionally not marking on student papers. She explained her new focus—finding positive things to talk about in student papers before negative things. She was surprised to see how much there was that was positive about her students' writing— things she hadn't been able to see before due to her prescriptive stance. Throughout her class, Julia marveled at her new teaching self and laughingly described how she had put aside red marking pens which she had used for sixteen years.

> *Julia:* I did look for good things and I did find them [laughs]. I mean they were there. "God, these aren't such bad writers after all. They can really make sense."
> *Researcher:* That's an interesting switch for you?
> *Julia:* Yeah. It was. For me. For sixteen years I've been, I was just taught to mark everything in red ink and that's it [laughter].

Such change, however, was not simple. During the course of her fall 1987 writing class, Julia did mention continuing evaluation concerns and problems, for instance, evaluating multiple draft papers and explaining her methods to colleagues. She also discussed struggling with the sense of herself as someone who would always care, to some extent, about surface correctness, for she was formerly the high school teacher who "loved" to teach grammar. Still, by the end of the her fall 1987 writing class, Julia was able to see that her new evaluation methods and classroom model were better for her and for her students.

Julia's vocabulary also changed. Instead of using grammatical jargon and expecting students to understand it, she began to use simple, paper-specific grammar or usage explanations. This change in vocabulary was mirrored by a change in self-perception. Julia wished she had recorded the student-centered vocabulary and explanations she used in her fall 1987 writing class because "a grammar teacher would probably go bananas" hearing her search for whatever explanation "worked" for her students rather than imposing grammatical terminology for discussions of their writing.

Julia and Change
The smaller area of how Julia addressed teaching grammar in her fall 1987 class reflected the larger pattern of change she underwent during the time of this research. At the beginning of the

Teaching Basic Writing seminar, summer 1987, Julia saw herself as an individual who enacted classroom change according to her mood. For some time, Julia had seen herself as someone too old to change. Although she doubted her ability to change, she hoped she would change. In the same way, she would respond somewhat conservatively to the material presented by Tom Bridges in the training seminar. She pointed out that she had to modify what he gave to her because it would be "difficult for me to let go." As the TBW seminar progressed, Julia continued to discuss her teaching methods. A sense that she might not have been so traditional, so prescriptive, so teacher-centered, started to surface. Midway through the summer pedagogy seminar, Julia saw herself as semi-prescriptive rather than as totally prescriptive, and, reflecting back on her past teaching, she realized her students had often evaluated her as very student-centered. What she was discovering through her pedagogy seminar enrollment and reflective learning log entries were the many new ways she could become even more student-centered in her classroom.

One real impediment to change for Julia seemed to be her worry about saving face with students—about not doing anything they would find foolish or inexplicable. "I'm thinking, personally, how am I going to, how am I going to appear to my students?" She also worried about departmental requirements that certain materials be taught and certain books used, and so on. She described her early years of teaching as being heavily concerned with covering materials, and she finally rebelled against her own conformity by saying, "And that's another thing I'm not going to do this year. I'm not going to try to finish the damn book." In order to move to a student-centered classroom model, Julia needed to rebel against her own good behavior wherein she taught as her model teachers taught and did everything required by department guidelines.

Midway through the training seminar, as Julia was reevaluating herself as "teacher-who-changes," she realized more fully how much she already had changed over the years, even before she enrolled in the doctoral program. Her formerly solid lecture classes had already started to include student writing groups and interactive discussions. At one point, Julia mentioned age as a change factor—she was getting older, getting soft, getting more lenient, getting mellow—she was becoming less demanding and rigid, but she mentioned these attributes almost as if she thought she had gotten easier on students because she was lazy. At the end of her fall 1987 writing class, she termed herself as having made a "big jump," and she no longer voiced some of her earlier fears about losing face in a student-centered classroom. She felt that sometimes she conducted a class the way she did out of a *new* sense of duty—that of duty to the Teaching Basic Writing seminar model, but she had also come to understand that holding back and being less prescriptive was not being lazy, was not a matter of not participating. Her feelings here are reminiscent of Janet Emig's observation (also quoted in Nick's case study) that "it's not self-abnegation. To me, it's extremely arrogant to decide not to participate" (1983, p. 133), and to decide, instead, to orchestrate a student-centered classroom.

Julia found that standing back to allow students to "discover" their own writing and usage patterns was, in some ways, more work than telling them what to do. Her insights in this area, after her fall course was completed, were particularly impressive.

Researcher: In your second interview [summer 1987], your real fear was of letting go to a student-centered class and I wondered how you felt about that now [fall 1987]?

Julia: Yeah. I did. But I don't have that fear now. You know I had this fear of not being, of not—if it were not teacher-centered then I wouldn't be in control [laughs]. And I don't know, but, and I'm just being real honest with you now. I did feel that there were times that I was, that I was sort of doing something because I knew it was the right thing to do. I didn't necessarily agree with it, but I did it because it made the students feel better. And, you know, it would be much quicker for me to say, just to pick up the paper, which is what I've been doing for years, to pick up the paper and say: "This is not a sentence, right? This is a sentence fragment. Do you understand why this is not?" But, I had to say something like: "You know Jimmy. This is a pretty good paper and I like your idea." And you know it took me, and I had to do all this prep before I finally got around to: "Did you see anything in this paper that didn't—look at how nicely this first part flows. Did you see anything in here that doesn't flow too nicely, that doesn't make too much sense with everything else?" And then I would go on to say: "Well why don't you read a little bit of it. Just read it out loud." It would be so much easier to say, "Look Jimmy [laughter]. This is not a sentence right here and you need to know. I want to tell you why this is not a sentence." So I had to do lots of, and I didn't mind, I liked doing those, I guess. It was another way I could get close to students too. Because they like hearing that you like their work.

The most dramatic areas of growth for Julia were in her changed vocabulary for talking about students and her attitude toward these students. Early on, Julia called herself a "mother-hen" to her students. Throughout interviews, she'd talk about students as kids. Certainly other teachers in the case studies used this term once or twice, but never to the extent that Julia used it. Julia also tended to use affectionate diminutives: "My little student in high school" who wrote "little" pieces, and so on. She did this, in part, because she "felt much older than they [students]—in terms of *wisdom*." For this reason, Julia, in previous semesters of teaching, had never shared her own writing drafts in class. She also sometimes worried, like Peg in another case study, that students weren't responsible enough, that they were "slick" at getting out of work or that they were too grade conscious.

By the time Julia had instituted the new writers' workshop approach in her fall 1987 writing classroom, she was recording a dramatically reversed view of her students. She believed this class represented the first time she had "treated these students as human beings." In fact, she had become so sensitive to the idea of her writers being equals and *peers* and to her classroom as the forum for the development of *all writers*' abilities that she was hesitant to institute a writing editorial board (as discussed in the TBW seminar)—one that would consist of students strong in usage skills who would help weaker students proofread their papers. She was not willing to draw public distinctions between strong and weak student writers. "You know, I don't know how to do that [institute an editorial board]. I mean, I'm afraid of, you know, I don't want anybody to think that I think one person is a better writer than the other, that we're not all in here in the same boat, that we're not all here working together."

Near the end of her fall 1987 class, Julia had also lost some of her worries about grading, claiming that she "wasn't giving them credit for being mature." She also appeared to be calling them "kids" less often and noting the shift herself. "I do see them [students] differently. Not just [as] little kids who are real dumb and don't know anything." Both she and her students reacted positively to a class-room where student writers were also treated like adult writers. Keeping these developments in mind, it is now useful to look at Julia's writing class, fall 1987.

Julia's Home Institution and Writing Class

After completing her first summer of doctoral program course work and enrolling in the Teaching Basic Writing seminar, Julia returned to her home institution to teach a course titled English 101 Composition, a three-credit course described briefly in the catalog as "Instruction in the writing of themes." Julia's own course information handout augmented this description with a short introduction to the writing workshop focus of the class. "English 101 is a freshman composition course that focuses on the development of writing skills. This writing workshop will provide students with experiences in composing, moving from inner world experiences to more academic writing throughout the course. Small group (peer evaluation) work and conferencing with the teacher will be used extensively in this course." This introduction was originally developed for Julia's curriculum guide and rationale, her final project for the Teaching Basic Writing seminar.

Class Assignments

Julia was able to use her Teaching Basic Writing seminar curriculum guide with few changes, indicating that she had effectively visualized her fall 1987 course, and that, unlike Nick in a previous case study, she did not mind following a preordained teaching plan. In fact, because of her heavy teaching load of five regular sections and two overload sections, she found such preplanning invaluable.

During a summer interview, Julia mentioned that the curriculum guide was about 80 percent real. She chose, however, not to emphasize in that document some of the class readings required by her department, a focus she knew Tom Bridges would not favor. Even when she described class readings with what she considered a light hand, Bridges's final comments on her curriculum guide reflected his concern that she stick to the writing workshop model. "Think of the writing workshop as the basic organization, students working individually or in groups while the teacher conferences. Don't let the readings overpower the class time. Otherwise, a full job [outlining a curriculum]," he wrote on her paper.

Each week of Julia's fall writing class was focused on topics such as conferencing, the research essay, composing, modes (because of English department expectations that students know how to narrate, define, classify, analyze), revising, editing, and choosing writing for the class magazine—all interspersed with ongoing writers' workshop. It was clear that the overall student-centered focus of Julia's class was set early in the semester. Julia described one student's decision to drop after the first day of class.

> *Julia:* I had one guy drop the first day. He was kind of awed. He asked me the first day, "So this is kind of self-paced? Self-paced learning?" And I said, "Well, I didn't want to say that because that sounds like something you just do on your own totally," which is what I told him. And I said, "I do not intend to leave you alone. And I intend to be with you every step of the way. So I don't really think we can call this self-paced."

Grades for Julia's class were computed from a writing portfolio, although individual papers were graded as they were turned in. These grades, however, were not recorded and the final portfolio grade overruled any previous evaluation. Julia was worried that students might lose papers and she emphasized their responsibility for keeping the themes and resubmitting them at the end of the semester. Because of her course load of seven classes, Julia did not even enter the grades in her gradebook (as she thought she might for protection), but students did not lose any papers through the semester.

Required writing in Julia's class was a blend of her own preferences and department requirements. Of the five final themes submitted for evaluation, two, by English department decree, needed to be themes about literature. Julia had mixed feelings about these themes. They interfered with her use of the Bridges assignment generator as a heuristic to help students brainstorm for topics and audiences for papers based on their own experiences and suited to their own interests. Julia also knew her students would be entering English 102 the next semester if they were successful in her class; English 102 was a composition class devoted wholly to literary study and explication. Because of those requirements, Julia included required literature themes and regular readings from the class reader, although she allowed less time than ever before for discussion of those readings—generally asking the groups to briefly review them or pointing to the readings as possible models to generate topics.

Students were shown how to use the assignment generator, and they developed three theme topics. Each paper was drafted, critiqued by peers and teacher, redrafted, and finally turned in to the teacher for grading. Students kept all themes and drafts and sometimes abandoned one topic and began another. In Julia's fall class, these themes were turned in at the students' discretion, a plan that resulted in some student procrastination. By the end of the semester, Julia was limiting the number of themes she would accept to one a week, to keep from being overloaded and to try to pace students.

Writing Evaluation

Writing evaluation in Julia's class included a mixture of peer and teacher review and conferencing, and a mixture of traditional teacher grading and less traditional final portfolio evaluation. First drafts were critiqued in groups and in conferences with the teacher, and students began to keep process charts, which encouraged them to consult many readers and to complete several drafts. Students prepared the next draft for workshop at their own pace, and then convened a conference with Julia, who might then encourage them to submit a final draft for grading or to continue drafting. There were no teacher-written comments on the first drafts.

Julia described her own evaluation process in a letter to me, written in the fall of 1987.

In the papers I'm sending you, you will probably not find very many valuable teacher comments—you see, I feel that by conferencing with them and talking through their problems, different avenues for writing, etc. (most of the time, they are jotting things down as we talk—which I recommended and you will note on their rough drafts), students should be able to determine the mistakes made or, the other side of the coin, the good writing they've done. . . . I don't need to harp on something that was supposed to be corrected—therefore, I simply write in the margin—LOC [lower order concerns—punctuation, spelling, etc.] or HOC [higher order concerns—organization, development, etc.]. It's interesting, I have very few HOCs to write. We are able to clear some major points of discussion before they are into finalizing drafts.

In some early class notes Julia also discussed her new evaluation measures with some wonder and pleasure. "9/23 Small group—peer evaluation of first draft. Boy, what a temptation for me to put in commas, capitalize words as I went from group to group looking at these papers. You know, usually (in the past) I would have collected these Draft 1 papers, red inked them all up—I really had to restrain myself—not really. Actually, I *enjoyed* looking at *what* these students had to say rather than just *how* they said it for a change. Was surprised, too, to see how well they write."

Early and late papers from Julia's class showed a minimum of teacher marking and no teacher summary on paper; this was consistent with her self-described evaluation procedures quoted above. Julia mentioned that summaries would take place in conferences with students.

Julia was happy with the new critiquing procedures that allowed her to carry her heavy course load and still offer her students valuable writing guidance. She commented that she was familiar with each paper before she ever came to grade it, having had several conferences with the student concerning each theme.

Final portfolios for each student included all graded essays, research paper, tests, and a photocopied page from a class journal which had previously received a grade. The portfolio was as much a summation of writing development through the class as it was a reevaluation of classwork. Julia reviewed each collection and affixed a final class grade.

A Typical Week

On the three hours (three classes) of video tape, Julia spent 75 percent of her time with the class convened as a writing workshop while she held individual conferences with students by moving from group to group and working with a student at the perimeter of that group. Other class time was devoted to regular segments (5 percent of class time) at the beginning of each class when students wrote in their journals and responded to peer journals. Julia expected students to begin this activity even before she arrived at the class. A slightly larger amount of time (10 percent) was devoted to teacher-led discussion, primarily of readings, and to discussions of writing process. During class discussion, Julia worked on her "wait time," trying to increase the amount of time she paused to allow for student responses to her questions. Teacher lecture (10 percent) in Julia's class often focused on the usage concerns she developed from checksheets of writing errors, noted as she evaluated final drafts of papers.

The peer groups were generally on task and did not require much monitoring from Julia. Students moved their chairs into small circles and the class noise level immediately rose. Julia visited each group in turn, drawing up a chair as she did so. Julia did mention wanting to spend more time with each class peer group, perhaps staying with a single group all class period in future semesters, to help focus their work and to spend better quality time with each group. She also verified the sense of class vocabulary (her use of higher order concerns [HOCs] and lower order concerns [LOCs] rather than traditional discussions of comma splice and subjunctive and antecedents, and so on). She said:

> And they, we had this real identification though with HOCs and LOCs and jokingly talked about it. But it was just so neat because they—it was just a nice way to abbreviate without having to talk about—you know—there is a punctuation error here, or there is a comma splice. Those words sound so harsh. One of my kids said that one day, he pointed out, "you know, I would much rather tell you, um, 'Ms. H would you come here and take a look at this LOC than to say to you, Ms. H, I need you to come over here and figure out where I've made, I think there's a *comma splice* [laughter].'" Yeah, it does feel better, you know . . . and I guess that's Tom Bridges's [terminology] isn't it? I need to write him a note and tell him that story.

Of the five hours of out-of-class time she devoted to this class, at the beginning of the semester Julia spent 60 percent evaluating student writing and 20 percent each on student conferences and class preparation. Near the end of the semester, though, her conference time doubled to 40 percent, reducing the time available for paper grading to 40 percent. Class prep time remained stable at 20 percent. Julia held conferences in her office, but she also encouraged students to call her. On the phone, they would ask questions and even read entire drafts aloud in order to receive her oral critique.

The following activities or techniques were important instructional focuses in the Teaching Basic Writing training seminar:

- Bridges assignment generator
  (or encouraging student-generated writing topics)
- peer writing groups
- sentence combining
- editorial board
- student journals or learning logs
- in-class student/teacher conferences
- teacher sharing his/her own writing
- publishing student writing
- formal measures to evaluate the writing classroom

Use of these activities and techniques was seen as supportive of the whole language, writing workshop classroom, as developed in the TBW seminar.

Julia used the *assignment generator,* as mentioned earlier, but added assigned themes (two literary and one research paper) to conform to department requirements. She felt the students responded well to the freedom to generate their own topics. The major planned change she foresaw was adding due dates to papers to keep students from procrastinating.

Peer work was another expanded focus in Julia's classroom. She used groups for brainstorming, drafting, and conferencing. She believed groups were effective, although she learned that her students worked best by staying in the same group for some time. She also noted that student groups registered a slight drop in enthusiasm late in the semester. She mentioned this in her class notes: "Noticed that concentration has dropped off in peer groups—seems that students are not putting the effort forth here toward the end of the semester in attempting to evaluate each other's papers." This lack of involvement might have been triggered by the assigned topics; she said students put off the literary analysis essays to the last. At the same time, she felt the students were doing a good job critiquing peer papers, particularly in the area of higher order concerns. Her plans for future classes included even more focus on small groups. She felt they were a better forum for usage instruction than the whole class discussion mode, where students ignored her or quickly stopped paying attention.

Julia consistently used *in-class conferencing* with positive results. She learned to prioritize her remarks, focusing first on positive aspects of student writing and also deciding not to mark on student drafts. Both of these techniques were major changes from her previous practices. She also continued to hold conferences outside of class and by phone. *Sentence combining* was used informally after a general class discussion. She asked students to make suggestions to each other for areas where they could combine sentences on papers. However, she felt that they didn't do a great deal with this. The class *editorial board* was originally planned but never implemented. At the end of her semester, Julia began to feel that it sent a contradictory message that some students were better than others, and she chose not to develop a board.

Julia collected student themes, intending to *publish student work*, but she did not do so due to her workload and time constraints. She did encourage students to submit their work to newspapers; several did and the work was published locally. A *structured class evaluation system* was not instituted either, primarily due to her heavy class load; however, Julia kept track of her class progress through several qualitative measures—a class reactionnaire, teaching notes and observations, and so on. She submitted class materials to me, accompanied by letters that discussed her class progress and her concerns and discoveries.

Journals were instituted in Julia's class, but she found that students wrote little without direct teacher prompting. She still found this activity valuable and planned for future semesters to institute out-of-class journal sharing groups similar to the one she participated in for the TBW seminar (as a learning log group member). For the first time in her teaching career, Julia *shared her own writing* with students and was impressed with their reactions. She also shared anecdotes about her own writing for newspapers. Overall, Julia expressed a strong positive response to the new classroom model she had developed, claiming she hoped never to lose her commitment to it.

Students confirmed this picture. This classroom, from teacher and student perspectives, encompassed a number of the techniques and activities proposed in the Teaching Basic Writing seminar and they were continued throughout the semester. Julia seemed to take Bridges's suggestion on her curriculum guide to heart as she moved the class focus from reading and discussion to the conference-based, writers' workshop—so much so that she received requests from students on the class reactionnaire to discuss the readings in more depth. In this classroom, peer activity and teacher conferences seemed to be in a functional balance, occurring simultaneously, with neither receiving disruptive prominence.

Discussion

In spite of her long career as a teacher of grades eight through sixteen, Julia entered the doctoral program relatively unacquainted with the scholarship and research in the field of compositions studies, particularly at the college level. She was a member of the National Council of Teachers of English but had subscribed to *English Journal* for more years than *College English*. Before entering the doctoral program, she had read few, if any, of the works by the scholars and teachers she would be introduced to during her graduate enrollment. Because of her lack of scholarly background, Julia did not appear to ascribe strongly to any particular teaching ideology, other than to claim that she began teaching when grammar was a focus of English and with a model teacher who was strong in that area. In spite of many years in the teaching profession, she remained somewhat of an outsider to a new and changed composition scene that Corbett (1987) describes. "The most salient feature of the current scene is the enhanced professionalism and the elevated status of the young composition teachers" (445). Corbett attributes this new professionalism and enhanced status to teachers' participation in teacher training programs and national organizations, arenas Julia was just entering.

At the same time, Julia was not a blank slate. She expected to change through her enrollment in the doctoral program, and in previous years she had already reduced the formal teacher-lecture format of her class, introduced peer work and I-Search papers, and questioned her own use of red marking pens. Unlike Peg, in another case study, who entered the program looking for revitalization and

who expressed a strong intent to discard all former teaching practices and to find a new best way of teaching, Julia seemed to enter
the program as a more generalized act of exploration while she
worked to complete the higher degree she had always expected to
pursue.

Julia's journey through the Teaching Basic Writing pedagogy
seminar and her return to her classroom with a new teaching
method reflected a different kind of conversion to process methodology than that of other case study teachers—for instance, Peg who
made a determined conversion or Nick who made a strong affective
and verbal conversion but who lost some practical momentum the
second half of his semester. Julia's conversion reflected in a more
complete manner the schematic "conversion" model of Crocker,
Fiske, and Taylor (1984), mentioned in previous case studies. What
at first appeared to be a bookkeeping type schema change—new
information gradually being assimilated in a series of adjustments,
as Julia added portfolio evaluation to her classroom, increased her
use of peer groups, and started using in-class conferencing—finally
resulted in a radically altered fall classroom: a writers' workshop
where 70 percent to 80 percent of the class time was devoted to
peer groups and teacher conferencing. The change in Julia's classroom model also led to changes in her traditional grading methods.
What appeared to be, at first, only slightly incongruent teaching
information became, by the time Julia compiled her curriculum
guide, "salient, dramatically incongruent instances" resulting in a
drastic teaching revision (p. 206). Crocker, Fiske, and Taylor note
that conversion schemas usually do not come into effect until another schema is available to replace the old one, and this would
certainly be the case in the Tom Bridges-taught pedagogy seminar
where a teacher like Julia, without strongly or rigidly held previous
beliefs, was offered a convincing new instructional model.

One of the striking changes that occurred in Julia's classroom was
the way she reconceptualized students as adult writers, capable of
mature writing. This reconceptualization seems closely aligned to,
and possibly dependent upon, her reconceptualization of her role as
a teacher. During her fall 1987 writing class, Julia moved from seeing herself as a grammarian to seeing herself as not-a-grammarian.
Julia entered her fall 1987 classroom with a new outlook and a new
vocabulary. Her vocabulary for discussing writing (higher order concerns and lower order concerns) and writers (peers and collabora-

tors) did not appear to be an overlay on old practices—as seemed to occur to an extent for another case study teacher, Rosalyn—but rather appeared to be *the most appropriate way* to describe her classroom.

Another vocabulary change also seemed to lead, in part, to her reconceptualization of her students. Julia less and less often used the student/teacher distinction and more and more often used adult or peer or mature as descriptive terms. As the work by Munby (1987) suggests, teachers' metaphorical knowledge may be quite predictive of the reality of the classroom, and a change in Julia's description of her students led to a real change in classroom behaviors and expectations. This type of "transference" is illuminated by Lindley (1987) in an essay entitled "The Source of Good Teaching." Lindley, from a background of Jungian psychology, claims that the successful teacher taps the "student" in herself and the "teacher" in her student to transfer authority from teacher to student by the end of a semester. "But at some point, or rather at various points during the school year, if things have gone well, a final stage occurs: the student finds that her inner teacher is all she needs. She can do the work on her own" (p. 164). In essence, the successful teacher enables students to become successful self-learners. Julia's dramatic reconceptualization of students as "peers" and "adults" seems to signal a successful transference of authority from teacher to students.

Julia's newborn respect for her students as writers led her to value their writing and allowed her more often to work as the successful teachers in the Perl and Wilson study (1986) who "offer[ed] invitations to their students to become writers" (p. 258). The maturity of her students' responses to these invitations supported and demanded her new paper evaluation methods. No longer did Julia turn white paper red with corrections; in fact, she no longer wrote on early drafts at all. Knoblauch and Brannon's study (1984b) found that students did not respond to even the most detailed and meticulous of summary comments. Julia seemed to discover this fact for herself, going farther than any other case study teacher in eliminating terminal markings and with her final grading of papers taking place primarily verbally, during conferences. She developed an evaluation procedure consistent with her new classroom model of instruction, one which no longer kept her up grading until 2:00 A.M. and dreading the start of each semester; it was a procedure that did not sap her teaching energy. Given Julia's regular five-course teaching schedule and her two-course overload fall 1987, these were important developments.

The one area that Julia didn't alter radically was the inclusion of class readings in her syllabus. Students themselves pointed out the inconsistency of giving them assigned readings that the workshop model left no time to cover. Knoblauch and Brannon (1984a) point out that different methodologies inserted into the same curriculum can give students mixed and conflicting messages about classroom values. This may have happened in Julia's classroom, although the shift to a workshop classroom was nearly complete. Due to department requirements, Julia still spent time teaching modes of discourse and reviewing model readings, and she required literary response papers.

Even while instituting many new classroom practices, Julia's class was well-organized. She mentioned in interview that she had a reputation for being a tough but fair teacher, and at the end of the semester, she felt she had not lost face with students by introducing new and possibly threatening teaching practices. Her sense of herself as classroom peer did not lead to a loss of identity or diminish her power to facilitate classroom activities and keep peer groups on track. Quite the reverse, her sense of discovery in the classroom and her enjoyment of her students in their new guise of adult writers, interesting *and* interested, lent energy to what might have been a daunting course load. She felt she was able to be personal and involved with students without needing to be dominant. At the end of seven class sections in the fall of 1987, Julia acknowledged continued and wholehearted conversion to her new classroom model.

> *Researcher:* Well, you sound like you've survived pretty well.
> *Julia:* Yes. And I like it much better. I feel better about my students and I feel better about my teaching, about being more positive.

For Julia, methodological change resulted in important affective change; her positive feelings about students, her classroom, and the method, predicted continued classroom development of the whole language, writing workshop as an effective teaching model for both her and her students.

7

College Writing Teachers and
Classroom Change

I am what I am, or I am nothing. I cannot think, reflect, or judge about my being, without starting from the very point which I aim at concluding. My ideas are all assumptions, and I am ever moving in a circle. I cannot avoid being sufficient for myself, for I cannot make myself any thing else, and to change me is to destroy me. If I do not use myself, I have no other self to use. My only business is to ascertain what I am, in order to put it to use. . . . What I have to ascertain is the laws under which I live. My first elementary lesson of duty is that of resignation to the laws of my nature, whatever they are; my first disobedience is to aspiration after what I cannot be, to cherish a distrust of my powers, and to desire to change laws which are identical with myself. (John Henry Cardinal Newman, quoted in Blehl, 1963, p. 317)

In "An Essay in Aid of a Grammar of Assent," the nine-teenth-century theologian, John Henry Cardinal Newman, described the ways individuals strive to develop religious certainty and the difficulties involved in change when humans are presented not with sufficient "scientific" evidence, but with the more usual "insufficient" evidence. Newman explored "how one can believe what one cannot fully understand" (Newman, quoted in Blehl,

1963, p. 285). A century later, although not struggling directly with questions of *religious* identity and *religious* belief, writing teachers in this study were striving to change their essential teaching identities and beliefs. Often, these teachers needed to take composition theory and the advice of their teacher trainer "on faith" until they tried a new teaching method in their classrooms and reconciled it to their "nature." Notably, they used religious metaphors to describe the intensity of their change process. They "confessed" to teaching grammar prescriptively. They marveled at their leaps of faith, and they announced that they were "converted" to process instruction. As participant-observer in the pedagogy seminar, I took field notes that recorded how the seminar was similar to a church revival meeting. The teacher trainer, Thomas Bridges, talked in interviews of moments when his seminar participants were "coming together," with teachers giving "testimony" in front of the "congregation." Not surprisingly, religious metaphors came naturally to these, often literature trained, adult learners as they underwent a powerful change process. Wilson (1988) reported similar, religious conversion metaphors occurring among teachers who participated in the Iowa Writing Project summer institute.

And Newman's work elegantly traces the struggles individuals undergo to achieve self-knowledge. In this study, teachers' disobedience to "duty" sometimes took the form of ignoring the pressures of state mandated proficiency tests or English department "rules," or even learning to subdue and modify their own teaching personalities. In the course of my observations, I was able to see these teachers work seriously to "change laws which are identical with myself." To do so, they tried teaching activities that were sometimes new and uncomfortable, like peer group work. They attempted in-class conferencing, placing themselves in a vulnerable position as they read and responded to student work on the spot. Equally, several were willing to confess to students that they weren't sure what they were asking for in the classroom would actually work. However, conversion metaphors really pointed to an underlying issue: How do teachers, and individuals, create and maintain social, professional, and personal identities? These teachers allowed me to observe the "business" of identity re-formation, a complex merging of old and new. And my conclusions here draw from composition studies, psychology, and sociology in order to offer some possible interpretive lenses for understanding these teachers' worlds; for as I studied each case, I came to agree more and more with Erik Erikson who claims, "'The study of identity . . . becomes as strategic in our time as the study of sexuality was in Freud's time'" (Erikson, quoted. in Stevens, 1983, p. 59).

Teachers as Learners

Janet Emig reminds us that it is "magical thinking" to expect students will learn directly what we teach them (1983). The same is true for teachers as learners when they become "students" in a pedagogy seminar like Teaching Basic Writing. Because teachers as learners are, foremost, complicated human beings, their development and change, in the Teaching Basic Writing seminar and after they returned to their own writing classrooms, reflected an interactive process which included affective, cognitive, *and* pedagogical development in patterns that were not easily isolated (and which probably should not be).

The Teaching Basic Writing classroom developed a convergent theory model of learning, with Tom Bridges, the seminar instructor, propounding a research- and theory-based "informed" writing classroom design that he hoped teachers would accept, adopt, and implement—that of the whole language, writing workshop classroom. Nevertheless, teachers in this study filtered all their learning through personal constructs that affected the way their classrooms actually developed during the fall of 1987.

Private and Public Teaching Theories

Several research studies support this view of teacher change. Swanson-Owens (1986) found the teachers in her study had "natural sources of resistance" to curricular change (p. 72). Perl and Wilson (1986) found that "how teachers interpret what they see in front of them determines how they act and how they teach" (p. 258). Parker (1988) explained the development of teachers-as-theorists in this manner. "Their personal theories do not necessarily, or even frequently, match closely with public theories. No one who works with teachers can assume that they espouse and act in terms of explicit, public paradigms. Rather, understanding individual teachers' methods of teaching requires understanding the personal, even idiosyncratic, theories that lie behind these methods" (p. 24).

Ethnographic research, then, was an ideal vehicle for allowing me to describe this complex set of interactions, and this study resulted in a rare look into the experiences of college teachers as they explored their *private theories* of writing instruction through training seminar discussions, learning logs, learning log groups, and pedagogy seminar projects. Additionally, they interacted with *public theories* of writing instruction as set forth by the teacher trainer, Tom Bridges, and as found in the seminar readings, drawn from current composition theory. In the case study teachers' own classrooms, it became evident that private and public theories underwent negotiation and modification.

Parker (1988) goes on to refer to the work of psychologist George Kelly (1963). Kelly's work allows us to imagine the order behind what can, at times, appear to be nothing more than individual teachers' idiosyncratic adoption of, or reconceptualization of, or resistance to public paradigms or theories. Parker explains:

> A person's constructs "channelize" her choices, decisions, and actions within particular areas of experience. These constructs form sets of pathways along which the person takes action and interprets events. A person's network of personal constructs, which can be construed as her personal theory, controls her thought and actions. And, to the extent that a person's constructs are unarticulated and unexamined, or are impermeable, that person is locked into particular ways of acting and interpreting the world. On the other hand, if a person's constructs are permeable, and, if they are articulated and examined, that person may undertake a liberating reconstruction of her perspective. As Kelly reminded us, events do not come to us bearing labels on their backs. We create the labels and the interpretations, and thus we remain free to reconstrue both. (pp. 24–25)

In order to understand how teachers in this study construed and reconstrued materials from the Teaching Basic Writing seminar and to understand which teachers' constructs appeared to be permeable or impermeable, it was necessary to study the teachers *in context*. As they entered the doctoral program, teachers brought constructs with them, and during enrollment in the doctoral program, forces from outside the seminar affected teachers' learning. In the Teaching Basic Writing seminar, seminar forces affected teachers' learning. And then, in their own, fall 1987, writing classrooms, matches were created between public theories and paradigms and each teacher's private teaching theory, or what Wittrock (1987) calls a teacher's "worldview." Wittrock claims, and this research verifies, that "change in teaching comes about not through [teachers accepting] individual research findings but through changes in the worldviews of the teachers and learners" (p. 377). Such changes occurred to differing extents for Susan, Rosalyn, Peg, and Nick, and occurred most dramatically for Julia.

Schema theory may give insights into how these worldviews are actually developed as information is presented in a pedagogy seminar. Each teacher took material from the seminar and processed it differently. Work by Crocker, Fiske, and Taylor (1984) in this area points to the influence of personal schemas on information storage, development of belief, and resistance to change. For instance, those with more expert knowledge in an area may have trouble assimilating, storing, and using "disconfirming" information since they have a greater investment in preexisting information. Therefore, an individual who believes students learn writing in a developmental progression and who has studied the research of developmental psychologists and compositionists like Piaget, Bruner, or Moffett, may have difficulty assimilating the work of non-developmental compositionists like Harste, Woodward, and Burke or Frank Smith.

Private and Public Identities

These teachers negotiated teaching theory and processed and stored large amounts of new information. They also were forced to negotiate their own developing identities. Brooke's (1988) work on writers' identities is useful here. He draws on the work of sociologist Goffman (1959, 1968), and psychologists Erikson (see Stevens, 1983), and Laing (1969), to define identity formation this way.

> An individual's identity, in other words, is a consequence of the way that person acts around others. On the basis of their actions (occupation, hobbies, mannerisms, quickness or slowness to anger, likes and dislikes, etc.), individuals come to be recognized and come to recognize them-

selves as certain sorts of people. This mutual recognition of self by self
and others becomes one's identity. In interacting with others, then, one
negotiates and is assigned a kind of consistent stance toward the world,
based on the pattern of one's past and present interactions. This assigned
consistent stance is, as far as anyone in the situation can tell, one's identity. (p. 24)

According to Erikson, the concept of "identity" includes personal or
"ego" identity and public identities. Stevens (1983) explains how
"Erikson conceives of identity as *psycho-social*. 'We deal with a process "located" *in the core of the individual* and yet also *in the core
of his communal culture*'" (Erikson, quoted in Stevens, p. 61). It is
sufficient to say that these teachers were constantly negotiating both
private and public concepts of their identity. And such identity negotiation can be exceedingly complex, as in Nick's case study. Additionally, identity negotiation involves teachers in social-cultural
struggles. From a Marxist/Freirean perspective, Giroux (1981) suggests such negotiation should be performed explicitly:

> That prospective teachers be given the concepts and methods to delve
> into their own biographies, to look at the sedimented history they carry
> around, and to learn how one's own cultural capital represents a dialect-
> ical interplay between private experience and history. Methods of cur-
> riculum design, implementation, and evaluation must be seen as a con-
> struction in values and ideology. This approach provides the foundation
> for future teachers to analyze how their own values mediate the class-
> room structures and student experiences they work with. (pp. 158–159)

Goffman's work suggests that such negotiation *may not* be
avoided. "Without something to belong to, we have no stable self,
and yet total commitment and attachment to any social unit implies
a kind of selflessness. Our sense of being a person can come from
being drawn into a wider social unit; our sense of selfhood can arise
through the little ways in which we resist the pull. Our status is
backed by the solid buildings of the world, while our sense of personal identity often resides in the cracks" (p. 320). For instance,
these teachers were always negotiating their public identities as
"students" in a doctoral program in rhetoric. They acted as teachers,
yet at a distance from their classroom; they acted as first-year or

"senior discourse" doctoral students; they acted as students *and* as friends to graduate program professors; and they acted as competitors in graduate studies and as collaborators in graduate studies with peers.

Private identities included teachers' being parents and/or spouses, and many had non-teaching or non-graduate school identities—as creative writers, or bicycle or music enthusiasts, sportspersons, and so on—but all at a distance from their normal practicing communities of such pursuits and personas. Equally, when they returned to their schools and their writing classrooms, the public identities that teachers negotiated were also complex. Some achieved new professional status and validation (and even moved to tenure-line teaching positions) due to their graduate course work in rhetoric: they were now seen by department heads, other teachers, and deans as "experts." At the same time, some worked to take on less authoritarian and more collaborative identities in the classroom.

The work of compositionists, psychologists, and sociologists, and even the work of a theologian like Newman, reminds us that the activity of teacher change—both trainers attempting to inculcate new teaching practices and teachers attempting to implement these new practices—is a taxing process of (re)theorization and (re)identification.

A Review of Classroom Change

The five case studies described here—those of Susan, Rosalyn, Peg, Nick, and Julia—pointed to a great number of factors that influenced each teacher's version of the whole language, writing workshop classroom. It should be noted that all five teachers instituted recognizable versions of the public paradigm of the Teaching Basic Writing seminar, which is praiseworthy, especially in view of the many complicated forces affecting their ability to develop this revised teaching "worldview."

Two case study teachers, Rosalyn and Julia, instituted workshop classrooms that appeared to most closely resemble the model developed in Tom Bridges's Teaching Basic Writing seminar. That model posited a classroom where, for 50 to 75 percent of class time, students, with the support of peer group members, wrote and critiqued multiple drafts of their own, self-generated essays while the teacher conducted individual conferences throughout the class period. Based on composition studies research, this classroom focused on writing fluency, clarity, and correctness, in that order; student engagement in the writing process, through self-generated topics; and the development of a classroom community of trust, based on the collaborative, peer work group model.

In the case study of Peg, this classroom model underwent an interesting reversal when Peg highlighted the individual conferencing element and backgrounded the peer work groups. In both Susan's and Nick's case studies, their classrooms were also more individualized and more teacher-directed than the TBW seminar "ideal" model. For instance, Nick's classroom appeared to begin with more of the ideal elements present and taper off somewhat as the semester progressed and his energy was devoted more often to out-of-class responsibilities.

In all five case studies, the public paradigm advocated in the Teaching Basic Writing seminar was modified by teachers' preexisting histories and personal teaching style or preferences and was influenced by their current estimation of student needs. This was not an unexpected development. As Langer and Applebee found in their 1987 study of pre-college level writing teachers, "We have also seen that it is relatively easy to introduce new writing activities into most classrooms, as long as these activities fulfill important pedagogical functions. Teachers will reinterpret such activities smoothly within the constraints and expectations governing their teaching. At the same time, however, process-oriented approaches to writing may contain the seeds of a more fundamental transformation in the nature of teaching and learning" (p. 87). In a similar manner, teachers in this study reinterpreted the Teaching Basic Writing seminar ideal model, and for at least two teachers, the model also "contained the seeds of a more fundamental transformation." The change process, then, was clearly transactional: some teachers adapted their learning, and learning transformed some teachers.

For instance, Susan's case study class was influenced by her estimation that the TBW model was already in effect in her classrooms and, yet, was not fully appropriate for her students. Her class was also affected by her past teaching history of individualized writing lab experience and her current responsibility for the entire pre-freshman level sequence at her college. Those factors led her to an apparently more structured classroom than that advocated in TBW.

In Rosalyn's case, her classroom closely resembled the model classroom of her curriculum guide, as developed for Teaching Basic Writing, with the personal inclusion of a broader and more structured method of grammar instruction and review. Rosalyn kept many of her previous methods even as she broadened and enlarged her classroom activities to introduce more workshop elements. In Peg's case, many of her previous classroom elements were abandoned at first, but her new model classroom moved back to her favored individualized approach, with the addition of extensive new evaluation procedures (portfolio evaluation, critique sheets, etc.). These, in turn, required a commitment of considerable evaluation time from her. Her previous lack of acquaintance with models of peer group development was not resolved in the Teaching Basic Writing seminar, and her ability to develop functioning peer groups proved to need further attention.

In Nick's case, his classroom was closer to the pedagogy seminar model when the semester began than when it ended. Nick was influenced by his love of classroom performance, his concurrent responsibilities for teaching speech and coaching the debating team, and his reliance on "energy" for carrying a classroom. These influences led him to a somewhat teacher-centered workshop; but his distaste for classroom planning and sticking to schedules and his heavy teaching load caused him to move away from his curriculum guide "contract" as the semester progressed.

In Julia's case, her classroom moved fairly quickly to the pedagogy seminar's workshop model due, in part, to her previous lack of strong commitment to a particular teaching model (although she had a strong previous commitment to grammar instruction). As she instituted her new teaching model, Julia gained a new respect for her students and developed better methods to manage a heavy evaluation load—and this created a positive and self-perpetuating class cycle. Julia, like the other case study teachers, was influenced by her previous strong commitment to grammar instruction and paper marking, but she was able to institute a unified classroom model that helped her rapidly change those habits and abandon some, although not all, of those influences.

Teachers in the five case studies did access pedagogy seminar information in personal yet definable ways. The models of schema

SUBTYPING (Susan)
TBW model is seen as believable but not appropriate. Stored for future use.

BOOKKEEPING (Rosalyn)
TBW model is seen as believable and stored in previously developed categories, broadening and widening categories. Previous practices/beliefs not necessarily abandoned.

INTENTIONAL CONVERSION (Peg)
TBW model is highly desired. Previous classroom model abandoned and new model adopted. However, it may not be possible to abandon previous practices/beliefs and unexpected previous teaching practices/beliefs reemerge.

VERBAL CONVERSION (Nick)
TBW model is highly desired and enthusiastically discussed. Implementation of new activities based on affect as much as on long-term cognitive/pedagogical planning. If energy drops, more taxing pedagogical practices may be dropped.

MULTI-FACETED CONVERSION (Julia)
TBW model is approached, evaluated and found believable. Initial integration of activities results in sudden new affect and practice and deeper cognitive understanding of model.

Figure 7-1. Summary of case study teachers' change pattens.

change mentioned earlier in all the case studies (Crocker, Fiske, Taylor, 1984) were just that—models. They provided me with a framework for identifying these teachers' different responses to the pedagogy seminar. Figure 7–1 builds on those models and expands categories. Clearly, a greater number of case studies would have resulted in both refined and expanded categories, for those categories listed by no means describe all possible patterns of teacher change.

Early in the Teaching Basic Writing seminar, Susan did appear to subtype the seminar information, marking it off as possibly (in fact, probably) valid, but not exactly applicable to her, perhaps for professional identity reasons. Rosalyn was the reverse. Because the course model was congruent to her needs, she adopted much of it. But she appeared to expand her methods as much as change them, using a bookkeeping model of many different categories to assimilate new amounts of information.

Peg intentionally converted to the seminar model. She was looking for nothing better than to adopt a more adequate method for teaching writing and for developing both her personal and her professional identities. It became clear in her case study that it may be more difficult than expected to abandon past influences. In fact, Peg did not abandon her previous most used teaching mode, one-to-one conferencing; instead, it became central once again to her class, with some resultant stresses.

Nick expressed conversion to the seminar model and indeed had an "ideal" model curriculum guide and rationale. His conversion rested on his affective state (energy level, enthusiasm) as much as on his class plan (cognitive and practical changes), and this affective conversion appeared to be highly dependent on outside influences. As Nick's affective state shifted, his class model shifted. For Nick, personal, professional, and social identity negotiation was extremely important and problematic.

Finally, Julia was more representative of conversion, in the traditional sense of the word, although during the Teaching Basic Writing seminar itself the conversion process was slow. She would confess to former poor (or no longer valued) teaching practices and decide to adopt one after another of the teaching modes and activities discussed in the pedagogy seminar. Once she was in her own writing classroom, the conversion was more rapid and thorough: Julia ended the semester with a new view of herself as a process paradigm teacher and with a different identity, that of not-a-grammarian. She also had a new view of her students, seeing them as peers and adults instead of as students and kids.

By the end of this study, some of the original research questions could be answered. For instance, teachers' preexisting attitudes toward or beliefs about composition *did* influence their willingness or ability to change through the course of a training seminar. And change patterns were neither simple nor predictable. Additionally, for all case study teachers, and presumably for all teachers enrolled in the pedagogy seminar, both short-term and long-term change occurred.

Simply put, these teachers had complex belief systems and pre-existing attitudes that influenced their ability to change. Described metaphorically, these were Giroux's "sedimented histories" (1981, p. 158). Teachers had orientations and attitudes toward composition pedagogy. For example, without exception, they viewed themselves as more process oriented than their colleagues and as open to change. However, teachers' orientations were only identifiable in general and on a continuum from current-traditional to natural-process, the two most mentioned "poles" in the composition studies literature. And as the training class progressed and case study teachers were interviewed, individual teachers developed their own idiosyncratic versions of the process paradigm, based primarily on their personal teaching histories and their perceived classroom needs. Hence, a teacher like Susan might advocate a structured process classroom while another like Rosalyn might institute a writing workshop classroom, with a hefty proportion of class time still devoted to grammar and usage instruction.

What becomes clear in such a discussion is that "theory" or "orientation" or "attitude" means one thing to the theorist who is positing an "ideal" model, as did Tom Bridges in the Teaching Basic Writing seminar, or as do Barnes and Shemilt in their suggested continuum of teaching, from transmission to interpretation (Parker, 1988). And it means another thing entirely to the practicing teacher who filters a theory through his or her reality and identity. In essence, each teacher "retheorizes" as he or she applies training classroom materials to her own classroom (Parker, 1988).

Additionally, while it became clear that teachers in these case studies viewed themselves as open to change, not all changed with the same intensity or in the same direction. Most teachers in the seminar and in the doctoral program (at least those in the summer sessions under study) portrayed themselves as "one who changes." These teachers perceived *dissonance* between their everyday teaching reality and a classroom ideal. They hoped to refine their pedagogy. For some teachers, such dissonance was strong. It led one teacher, Peg, to perhaps prematurely abandon her former classroom practices, many of which she later readopted.

To develop a new model of teaching, teachers needed to experience *congruence* between the training seminar model and their own classroom needs. Case study teachers Rosalyn, Peg, and Julia, for instance, appeared to experience congruence with seminar materials. And the model presented in TBW, while raising questions, finally seemed doable for these teachers and suited to their students' needs. For Susan, another case study teacher, and for Helen, a non-case study teacher who wrote to me to report her later feelings about the seminar, there was less immediate congruence between the training model and these teachers' perceptions of their current writing classrooms. Because they felt they already *had* developed process classrooms, they expressed less need to institute a new model and believed they had fewer practices to change. Finally, another case study teacher, Nick, saw the TBW seminar model as congruent but perhaps not doable. Early on, he wondered if he would have the expertise and energy to implement the many activities that he hoped to implement; as his semester developed, he truncated his ideal classroom plan due to unexpected out-of-class time demands.

Finally, teachers with considerable *tolerance* seemed to be able to refrain from judging the "fit" of seminar materials long enough to allow them to "believe" in the model classroom and to develop a workable curriculum guide. Their investments in their curriculum guides enhanced their classroom commitment to the new model, and the guide was shared with colleagues and administrators once these teachers returned to their institutions. This, *in turn*, committed them to the use of that curriculum guide as a classroom plan.

Teachers' tolerance was important inside and outside of the pedagogy seminar. Change for all teachers required that they maintain a high tolerance for ambiguity and for enduring the threats of identity loss or classroom chaos. Teachers needed tolerance as learners and as teachers. In the TBW seminar, they needed to trust Tom Bridges who asked them to suspend judgement and be believers as well as doubters while he led them to a convergent theory model of writing instruction. As teachers, they had to have tolerance for their own classroom behaviors and not require a perfect first implementation of new teaching practices.

Equally, teachers needed to be tolerant of their students who were also adapting to a new classroom model. This became evident in the case studies. Peg, a case study teacher who set perhaps unrealistically high standards for both herself and her students, had a low tolerance for what she judged to be poor student behaviors—students who "weaseled" out of work. Her attitude toward her students influenced her classroom development negatively. A second case study teacher, Rosalyn, had an initially high tolerance for freshman student behaviors. Her attitude toward her students influenced her classroom development positively. A third case study teacher, Julia, changed her attitude toward her students from a negative view to a positive view, with a resultant positive impact on her classroom development.

While teachers' attitudes in general were important, preexisting beliefs about and actual experiences with specific teaching practices also influenced the case study teachers. Nick, who did not like sentence combining and viewed it as a form of direct grammar instruction, never was evenhanded in his consideration of sentence combining research, and, he categorically refused to use it in his class. Less overtly, Peg's long-term commitment to individualized instruction seemed to obstruct her implementation of peer writing groups. She backgrounded peer groups because she was busy foregrounding conferencing.

The influence of teachers' preexisting beliefs about pedagogical activities was particularly striking in the area of grammar and usage instruction. Two case study teachers, Rosalyn and Julia, were particularly involved with this issue. Rosalyn did not choose to remove direct grammar instruction from her curriculum, in spite of a stated belief in research that showed it was not a productive use of class time. Instead, she instituted wider, more varied, and (she hoped) more process oriented methods of reviewing usage skills. Methods included using worksheets drawn from student writing, responding in this area in student journals, and so on.

Julia also continued to address grammar and usage in her class. Her long-held beliefs concerning the need for teacher intervention in this area *were* modified. She forced herself to suspend early marking (red-inking) of student papers and to look for content first, and she found to her surprise and delight that the content was there—and better than she had expected.

Short-Term and Long-Term Teacher Change

Teachers, as they left the Teaching Basic Writing seminar, had every expectation that long-term change had occurred in their views of teaching writing and in the directions they would take in future classrooms. One important insight into the duration of teacher change came from a non-case study teacher, Helen, who unexpectedly wrote to me during the spring 1988 semester to describe her post-pedagogy seminar teaching experiences. During the Teaching Basic Writing seminar, I had identified this teacher as somewhat resistant to change, an observation later confirmed by my analysis of her learning log (Bishop 1988, 1989). Helen felt she already knew and practiced in her college writing classes a great deal of what was being taught in the pedagogy seminar. She chaffed at Tom Bridges's seminar structure and teaching style. When asked to participate as a case study teacher, Helen felt she wouldn't have time to get involved since she was already being studied by a teacher-researcher at her home institution. However, several months after the seminar ended, Helen spontaneously reviewed her experiences in Teaching Basic Writing and found them profoundly influential in large and in small ways. An excerpt from her letter (spring 1988) follows.

When I spoke with you last summer, I explained that the community college at which I work has been using conferencing, student-selected assignments, group work, etc. for several years. Therefore, I saw the immediate worth of The Basic Writer [pedagogy seminar] as a reinforcement of what I was already doing. I know that I answered some of your questions with that reinforcement idea in mind.

When I left, I didn't expect to think much about the course. I was wrong. The effects of the assigned readings, Tom's class activities, and his comments began having a subtle influence on my classes and my division as soon as the first term began. . . . I think the biggest impact of Tom's class was on me. . . . I also felt much more at ease using write-to-learn activities in all my classes—particularly in my literature class. (I had begun this move before attending [Gatton University], but Tom's course gave me the incentive I needed to expand my activities.) My students wrote, and I wrote with them. We added dialog journals, computer bulletin boards, and classroom message centers to the activities I was already using.

I hope you have not drifted off by now and that some of this is making sense. Can you tell that as the pieces of the puzzle continue to fill in, I am becoming more and more excited about what I am learning? I just had to let you know that I gained more than reinforcement from Tom's course. In looking back at what I already have done, I realize how short-sighted my projected worth of the course was.

Assimilation of class learning and activities for Helen was a long-term process and occurred in spite of her not expecting any influence or change. It seems obvious, then, that teaching change, like writing change, is slow and convoluted. There is no clear developmental process which mandates that teacher change has to occur *during* a pedagogy seminar or during the teacher's first post-seminar writing class. Rather, this teacher, like Susan in a case study, appeared to have stored material, sub-typed it, and reactivated what she learned when is was required and *appropriate* (exhibited congruence). Teacher change, then, can occur unexpectedly and at a later date, the seeds for change still having been sown in the pedagogy seminar.

The reverse process also occurred. As "converted" teachers left the seminar and moved into their own writing classroom environment, they had to adjust their changes to their energy levels and to practical realities. Myers (1985) addresses this issue.

> In lesson design, the teacher is handling three sets of variables at once—the learner, subject matter or content, and school policy. Teachers, dealing as they are with sets of variables that often contraduct [*sic*] each other, soon learn that optimum solutions to problems, the luxury of planners outside the classroom, are rarely, if ever, possible in actual classrooms. Rather than aim for optimum solutions, teachers learn to aim for satisfices, a combination of what will suffice and what will satisfy. (Herbert Simon's *The Artificial Sciences* [*sic*], 1981, is the source of this term.) (p. 110)

Therefore, the way that case study teachers modified their ideal curriculum guides in their writing classrooms is not surprising. For instance, Rosalyn, responding to department mandated exit tests that consisted of *50 percent* of her students' class grades, *satisficed* on the issue of direct grammar instruction. Rosalyn did not abandon such instruction but broadened her approach and tried to make her methods more process-oriented and in keeping with her classroom model.

The five case study teachers in this research returned to their fall 1987 classrooms and earnestly proceeded to institute new curriculums. They were all successful to a certain extent, from their own "worldviews" particularly. In final interviews, all expressed satisfaction with their new classroom model and expressed strong commitment to refining their next class. Each expressed a sense that the first semester was truly a shakedown cruise, a first version, a class model in process. Success in their fall 1987 classrooms came in part from their newfound understanding of themselves as teaching professionals—insiders in the doctoral program discourse community and the composition studies profession. And even though these teachers had varying rates of success with their new model classrooms, all of them expected to continue to change and to improve their teaching in future semesters.

Clearly, for these teachers, change will continue to occur beyond the time-constraints of this study. Further research might profitably address such long-term change in longitudinal case studies that chart classroom activities over a multi-year period. It is important to discover more specifically the ways in which teachers construe, develop, and change teaching theories and the ways in which teachers' public and private identities evolve, for "*both* knowledge and people are 'processed' in schools" (Giroux, 1981, p. 157). And process classrooms, of necessity, implicate teachers in change.

Writing teachers are no longer expected to be at the center of the writing classroom. They are learning instead to stand supportively to the side and offer their students opportunities to grow and learn. However, writing teachers are central to writing students' development, and it is important, because of this, to understand how teachers approach their own learning in pedagogy seminars. The entire, complex enterprise they undertake deserves closer attention, for these teachers are at the heart of curricular improvement in our college writing classrooms.

Appendix
References

Appendix

Data Collection Strategies

Level 1
(Pre-study data)

1. I analyzed *Participant Evaluation Instruction* forms (PEI) for Teaching Basic Writing instructor, Tom Bridges, summer session 1986. (SURVEY)
   Survey instrument provided by Gatton University.
2. I completed a bibliographic search of research and literature for writing teacher training.

Level 2
(Collection of data from new doctoral program participants: Summer Session 1; study of Teaching Basic Writing seminar: Summer Session 2)

Summer Session 1

1. Tom Bridges collected TAWI: *Teacher Attitude Toward Writing Instruction* Survey for newly enrolling doctoral program participants during first meeting. (SURVEY)
   Measures teachers' process orientations (source: Gere, Schussler, & Abbott, 1984). For raw data, survey summaries, matrix displays, see Bishop, 1988.
2. Tom Bridges collected *Writing Apprehension* Survey (WAS) for

newly enrolling doctoral program participants during first meeting. (SURVEY)

Measures teachers' writing apprehension (source: Daly & Miller, 1975).

3. Tom Bridges collected Teaching and Writing History Survey from newly enrolling doctoral program participants during first meeting. (SURVEY)

Reviews teachers' past teaching and writing experiences (sources: Thompson, 1979; research questions).

Summer Session 2

1. I collected materials 1–3 above for any newly enrolling participant in the TBW seminar and doctoral program and for any participant who neglected to fill out such forms during the first session collection period (about 10 percent of participants). (SURVEYS)
2. As researcher, I acted as a participant-observer in the Teaching Basic Writing seminar, taking field notes and writing narrative summaries of each day's class, observing:
    a. group memberships,
    b. classroom behaviors and activities of both participants and instructor,
    c. relevant conversations,
    d. classroom setting, and so on.
       (Goetz and LeCompte, 1984)
    (PARTICIPANT-OBSERVATION)
3. I kept ongoing field notes to record the process of analysis, synthesis, summary, and description that is a continuous part of ethnographic data collection and analysis. (FIELD-NOTES)
4. I conducted weekly, taped interviews with the instructor to perform the following functions:
    a. reground weekly classroom observations, verifying and expanding my observations concerning the class culture;
    b. access the instructor's perceptions about class development and the instructor's attitudes toward the class;
    c. detail instructor's "class-view";
    d. review instructor's taped grading comments for teachers' final class papers (post Summer Session 2). (INTERVIEW)

5. I conducted and tape recorded scheduled, standardized interviews with seminar participants. (INTERVIEW)

    a. Interviews lasted approximately forty to fifty minutes and were scheduled during the first two weeks and the last two weeks of the seminar. Questions were semi-structured and sequenced (questions asked in the same order to address as many research questions as possible in a limited time frame) and included both closed and open questions (to allow for original, teacher-developed insights and conversational directions) (Goetz & Le-Compte, 1984).

       The first interview discussed teachers' previous teaching experience and their goals and expectations for the TBW seminar. Materials collected from the Teaching and Writing History survey helped in developing relevant questions.

       The second interview focused on the Teaching Basic Writing seminar (confirmational interviewing), the learning log groups, and the final paper.

       The second interview was also used to discuss the follow-up study with teachers in order to recruit teachers willing to be fall 1987 case study teachers.

    b. Eight teachers were identified as potential case study teachers on the basis of being employed, college level instructors of composition who were returning to their fall 1987 classrooms to teach pre-freshman and/or freshman composition classes in which they might be expected to utilize information gathered during their participation in the TBW seminar. Selection rested on teacher willingness to participate in the case study research project. Seven teachers (four female, three male) agreed to participate (the eighth teacher was already involved in a research project).

    c. Additional tapes of special interest or value were collected: interviews with advanced doctoral program participants, doctoral program instructors, learning log group meetings, and so on.

6. I collected copies of learning logs for all TBW participants and seminar papers for case study teachers, as well as all TBW seminar handouts and seminar readings and texts which provided data about the seminar structure, orientation, focus, and theoretical base. (ARTIFACTS)

7. Collection of *Methods and Theories* forms (M&T) and *Writing Re*search forms (WR). (SURVEY)
8. Collection of TAWI survey for seminar participants (last week of TBW seminar). (SURVEY)
9. Collection of *Participants' Evaluation of Instruction* forms (PEI) for Teaching Basic Writing, summer 1987.

Level 3
(Case-studies of five seminar teachers in their writing classrooms)

1. Participating teachers agreed to collect the following class artifacts:
   a. class syllabus, handouts, and texts;
   b. two sets of graded (or evaluated) papers from the entire class (one early set, one late set). (ARTIFACTS)
2. Teachers also collected a completed set of student questionnaires:
   a. Student Exposure Survey (SES), recording the classes' exposure to particular writing techniques emphasized during the Teaching Basic Writing seminar (source: Fulwiler, Gorman, & Gorman, 1986);
   b. Writing Apprehension Survey for entire class during first and last weeks of class. (SURVEY)
3. Teachers provided video and audio-tapes of three consecutive class sessions, beginning any time after the first third of the semester or quarter. (CLASS TRANSCRIPTS)
4. I conducted a minimum of two, tape recorded telephone interviews with each teacher regarding classroom practices. Interviews took place, approximately, during week 5 and weeks 12 through 15 of the fall 1987 semester. (INTERVIEWS)
5. Participating teachers retook the TAWI survey at the close of the fall 1987 semester. (SURVEY)

Figure A-1 summarizes data collection.

Data Analysis

The ethnographer must deal with multiple data sources and large amounts of complex and sometimes conflicting data in a reliable manner. She must label and record all data and then proceed to

	Level 1 Spring 1987	Level 2 Summer 1987*	Level 3 Fall 1987**	Level 4 Spring 1988
Bibliographic review— teacher training	Start			Continues
PEI Evaluations:				
Summer 1986	Copied and analyzed			
Summer 1987			Copied and analyzed	
WAS/TAWI Surveys		Week 1 & Week 10		
Writing & Teaching History Survey		Week 1		
Classroom written artifacts		Collected weeks 6–10 . . .		
Interviews:				
Instructor TBW		Collected weekly 6–10, with follow-up fall & spring (1987–1988)		
Participants TBW		Collected weeks 6–7 and 9–10		
Methods and Theories Forms (M&T):		Week 6		
Writing Research (WR):		Week 6		
Seminar papers and learning logs:				
Participants TBW		Week 10		
Informal Contact		Weeks 5–10		
Participant-observation		Weeks 6–10		
Researcher's field notes collected throughout		....		
Follow-up study:				
Class artifacts			Weeks 1–14	
Sample class papers			Early and late	
Student WAS survey			First & last weeks	
Class Video Tapes			3 classes, midsemester	
Teacher Interviews			Early and late	
Student Questionnaires (SES)			Late	
Teacher TAWI survey			Late	
Analysis		Start		Finish (1/89)

*Weeks 1–5 = first summer session; Weeks 6–10 = second summer session for doctoral program participants

**Weeks 1 (early)–14 (late) semester system or 1 (early)–9 (late) quarter system for case study teachers

Figure A-1. Data collection and study timetable.

analyze, reduce, reanalyze, reduce, and reanalyze data in a recursive fashion before presenting it clearly and graphically in research report format. To do this, she must develop collection and analysis procedures and follow them rigorously. McAndrew (1987) describes this demanding task. "Teachers and researchers who have conducted these naturalistic studies report that the amount of data collected can at times seem, and may in reality be, overwhelming. In order to record the natural events of writing classrooms calls for amassing an amount and a complexity of data that requires structured procedures to maintain control through the processes of data collection, analysis and interpretation" (p. 1).

The data collected in this study occurred in three mediums: print, audio tape, and video tape. My data analysis procedures for all three mediums follows.

Print Data

I developed a continuous record-keeping procedure so that all material was collected and filed for future use. Methods included: labeled and alphabetized file folders for all print data, from survey questions to TBW learning logs to seminar papers to the student papers in the TBW case study teachers' own classes. By the end of the study, I had amassed print artifacts that filled approximately two, four-drawer file cabinets. Other print data was generated throughout the course of the research. I kept records of case study materials to assure that each teacher's case study could be considered complete, logging in material as it was collected.

During my participation in the Teaching Basic Writing Seminar, I typed daily field note summaries and, often, reviewed and elaborated notes. I collected 157 pages of handwritten class observation notes and typed 74 pages of field note summaries during the five-week period of the second summer session. During the fall of 1987 and the spring of 1988, I kept analysis/writing notes on the microcomputer as I transcribed tapes, entering observations and sorting out themes and ideas. In these notes, I began the process of shaping the final research report and began data reduction, recording observations, points of interest, and problem areas in the materials I was reviewing and transcribing. I wrote approximately 50 pages of these informal notes. During the final writing of the research report, these computer notes were supplemented by handwritten note cards, developed primarily from learning log analyses and coding sessions. The notecards provided an informal index for the learning logs.

Audio Tapes

I conducted first-week and last-week interviews with thirteen participants in the teaching basic writing class. I conducted early fall semester and late fall semester interviews with five case study teachers. I recorded thirty-six hours of the forty-hour Teaching Basic Writing seminar; daily post-seminar interviews with the instructor, Tom Bridges; weekly summary interviews, also with Bridges; and a variety of interviews with professors, advanced doctoral program participants, learning log group meetings, and so on. I kept a written record of these interviews, including details of interview date, time, location, and other salient factors such as poor tape quality, etc. In total, seventy-nine hours of taping were completed.

Using a microcassette transcriber, I transcribed tapes, working from the center of the project—interviews with participants—outward: first all tapes by the case study teachers were transcribed, next all tapes by other TBW participants, all tapes with doctoral program professors, including the TBW instructor, and so on. Figure A-2 provides a sample transcription. I then reviewed and made notes on interviews with advanced doctoral program participants and for selected tapes from the TBW seminar. Use of the microcassette transcriber allowed for highly accurate transcription of the tapes on a word-for-word basis; however, I made no attempt to record voice modulation and all pauses and emphases (although I did indicate long pauses, heavy emphasis, and humor). Where faulty recordings made transcription difficult, I noted this information on the transcripts. A one-hour tape took nearly four hours to transcribe and resulted in approximately twenty-five pages of written data. Forty hours of tape were transcribed in this manner and resulted in approximately one thousand pages of written transcripts.

Interview transcripts were not coded. Instead, because the interviews with participants were structured and sequenced (Goetz & LeCompte, 1984) and, generally, the same questions asked in the same order for all participants, I was able to form simple matrix displays to overview participants' answers to any given question (Miles & Huberman, 1984; McAndrew 1987).

Note: First Interview. Short dash (–) = interviewer; longer dash (—) = participant
7/21/87

–Give me a who's who, sort of short bio, a little more detail in terms of what your training to be a teacher has been, where you've been teaching, to coming here, what got you here.

—Well, uh, I've been teaching high school English for sixteen years in a very rural school district in a very small tiny place in E—— County. And uh . . . this is my sixteenth year, my sabbatical year is my sixteenth year, I'm on sabbatical right now, or I was during the semester. Uh . . . and, uh, I have in retrospect, looking at my own teaching, have to classify myself as a staunch current-traditionalist, I mean that's what I what my background was. I had never heard of *any* of the names that are everyday conversation in our field, the names that have become second nature to me since I've been here. Um, I had no conception of what process writing was, uh, but, I knew that there was this program here and I knew that it was innovative.
–How did you know that?
—Uh, because I checked around. I wanted to work on a Ph.D.

Figure A-2. Sample tape transcription.

Video Tapes

Case study teachers were asked to collect video and audio tapes of three consecutive class periods in their writing classrooms. They collected these at their own discretion any time after the first three weeks of class when the class had progressed enough to allow the teacher to feel comfortable with the taping. The tapes that were collected were an important but highly variable data source. Video and audio taping quality ranged from primitive—poor sound and a fixed camera—to elegant—a well-trained operator who might include both teacher and students in the video frame (fixed cameras sometimes did not) and place separate microphones unobtrusively within each peer group work area. Although I asked the case study teachers to show as much as possible, to offer a window into his or her classroom, clearly these windows were not identical.

I reviewed the video tapes and took notes, much as I had when sitting in the Teaching Basic Writing Seminar. I commented on the atmosphere of each classroom and carefully noted drawbacks of the taping session. In final interviews with case study teachers, I questioned each teacher about what I had seen on the tapes, attempting to verify and expand my impressions.

Learning Log Coding and Analysis

It became apparent when reviewing the print data that the teachers' learning logs would provide a major source of information on teachers' learning in the TBW seminar. In order to deal with the massive amounts of data available in the learning logs, most of which did not fall into a logical or manageable sequence like that of the structured interviews, it was necessary to develop a coding system that would allow me to retrieve data and display it in an accessible format.

I divided learning logs into T-units and coded them with a set of codes developed from the instructions given to the participants in TBW which directed their log writing and from the research questions themselves. The codes are shown in Figure A-3. T-units, or terminable units, according to Hunt (1977) are "a single main clause (or independent clause, if you prefer) plus whatever other subordinate clauses or nonclauses are attached to, or embedded within, that one main clause. Put more briefly, a T-unit is a single main clause plus whatever else goes with it" (pp. 92–93). I tried codes on a few logs and refined them, conflating overlapping categories and eliminating null categories until I could recode the same log twice using the final codes, with a strong expectation of applying the same code each time to each T-unit. I either transcribed logs onto microcomputer and then coded, or I photocopied at a reduced size and coded on the photocopy. I chose to code learning logs myself, following the practice described by McCarthy (1987) in her study, "A Stranger in a Strange Lands: A College Student Writing Across the Curriculum." McCarthy explains her decision to code and analyze protocols. "I carried out the analyses of the protocols alone because of the understanding of the writing context that I brought to the task. I viewed this knowledge as an asset in identifying and classifying Dave's [case study student] writing concerns. Thus, instead of agreement between raters, I worked for 'confirmability' in the sense of agreement among a variety of information sources" (p. 241).

Equally, in the case of this research project, codes were intended to provide a general analysis of teachers' writing—subjects and fo-

Response Codes		Subject Codes	
REC:	record information or events	R:	readings
RES:	respond to information or events	C:	Teaching Basic Writing class
QUES:	question information or events	I:	instructor of Teaching Basic Writing
REHRS:	rehearse role or use jargon	LL:	learning log or log group
		S:	self-analysis
CONC:	connect information or events	T:	own teaching or teaching profession
CONSOL:	consolidate, summarize, interrelate systems and/or concepts	O-S:	other participants of Teaching Basic Writing
PRE:	predict future interactions of information or events	O-GP:	graduate program or composition profession in general
INVEN:	create new material from concepts/relationships	O-H:	teacher's home institution
A/S/L:	analysis/synthesis comments on writer's own learning (metacognitive comments)		
A/S/T:	analysis/synthesis comments on teaching of TBW (metateaching comments)		
A/S/W:	analysis/synthesis comments on writer's own writing (metalinguistic comments)		
REJ:	rejects information or events		

Figure A-3. Learning log codes: Used for log writers' entries.

cus. Additionally, learning logs confirmed other research data (survey questionnaires and interviews) and allowed me to learn more about what teachers observed about their learning *across* the logs. Once coded, the types of responses were tabulated and used to ana-

RES-R	I like Perl's explanation of "retrospective structuring" to clarify the recursive nature of making meaning./ She
RES-R	also does a good job in discussing the features of BWs that many of us have seen so often in our classes—role confusion, selective perception, egocentricity, etc./
CONC-T	But discerning these problems and doing something about them are two entirely different things./ Her first principle that teachers must identify which
RES-R	characteristic components of *each* student's process facilitate writing and which inhibit it before they can do any good is certainly sound./ [.I felt the
AGR-KEN	same way when I read it. Ken] It is also a very daunting challenge for each of us
CONC-T	to put into practice, given the constraints of our teaching situations./
RES-R	Flower. Writer-based prose. Flower really puts her finger on the BW complaint "I know what I want to say, but I just can't put it into words."/ The gulf between psychological meaning and reader-based
CONSOL-R	expression is a tough one to bridge for all but the most articulate of us;/ I can
RES-R	really empathize with those kids./ [.me
AGR-KEN	too. Ken]

Figure A-4. Extract from learning log for Reed, log group 1.

lyze response tendencies and patterns of group participants. Did one teacher *respond to* more than *analyze* class material? Did another teacher focus on her own classroom teaching while another focused exclusively on TBW readings and synthesizing those readings into an understanding of composition studies?

Additionally, because the logs were response logs—teachers responded to the entries made in group members' logs—I also evaluated peer response by a simpler coding system to try to analyze what role the peer took in general: was the peer supportive, challenging, questioning, etc.? The use of humor in response entries was also coded, as the use of humor was prevalent.

I coded thirteen learning logs, ranging from 25 handwritten pages to 105 handwritten pages and from 15 single-spaced typed pages to 66 double-spaced typed pages. The average learning log was 609 T-units in length. Therefore, approximately 7,917 T-units were coded. A sample section from a coded log appears in Figure A-4.

Survey Analysis

Survey material was collected in the form of likert-type scales for early and late testing of the pedagogy class and participants' own writing classes, and a few fill-in the blank questions were introduced during teacher interviews. Materials from these surveys was used for triangulation purposes, to verify interview or observational data.

References

Anson, C. M. (1989). Response styles and ways of knowing. In C. M. Anson (Ed.), *Writing and response: Theory, practice, and research* (pp. 332–366). Urbana, IL: National Council of Teachers of English.

Applebee, A. N. (1986). Problems in process approaches: Toward a reconceptualization of process instruction. In A. R. Petrosky & D. Bartholomae (Eds.), *The teaching of writing: Eighty-fifth yearbook of the National Society for the Study of Education* (pp. 95–113). Chicago, IL: University of Chicago Press.

Bartholomae, D., & Petrosky, A. R. (1987). Facts, artifacts, and counterfacts: A basic reading and writing course for the college curriculum. In T. Enos (Ed.), *A sourcebook for basic writing teachers* (pp. 275–306). New York: Random House.

Beaven, M. H. (1977). Individualized goal setting, self-evaluation, and peer evaluation. In C. R. Cooper & L. Odell (Eds.), *Evaluating writing: Describing, measuring, judging* (pp. 135–153). Urbana, IL: National Council of Teachers of English.

Berkenkotter, C., Huckin, T. N., & Ackerman, J. (1988). Conventions, conversations, and the writer: Case study of a student in a rhetoric Ph.D. program. *Research in the Teaching of English, 22,* 9–44.

Berlin, J. (1987). *Rhetoric and reality: Writing instruction in American colleges, 1900–1985.* Carbondale, IL: Southern Illinois University Press.

Bishop, W. (1988). A microethnography with case studies of teacher development through a graduate training course in teaching writing. Unpublished doctoral dissertation, Indiana University of Pennsylvania, Indiana, PA.

Bishop, W. (1989, March). *Teachers as learners: Negotiated roles in college writing teachers' learning logs.* Paper presented at the 1989 Conference on College Composition and Communication, Seattle.

Bissex, G. (1980). *GNYS AT WRK: A child learns to write and read.* Cambridge, MA: Harvard University Press.

Bizzell, P. (1986). Composing processes: An overview. In A. R. Petrosky & D. Bartholomae (Eds.), *The teaching of writing: Eighty-fifth yearbook of the National Society for the Study of Education* (pp. 49–70). Chicago, IL: University of Chicago Press.

Bizzell, P. (1987). Language in culture and cognition. In T. Enos (Ed.), *A sourcebook for basic writing teachers* (pp. 125–137). New York: Random House.

Blehl, V. F. (Ed.). (1963). *The essential Newman.* New York: New American Library.

Boirsky, C. (1980). A cognitive map for teachers of writing. *English Education, 12,* 77–87.

Braddock, R., Lloyd-Jones, R., & Schoer, L. (1963). *Research in written composition.* Urbana, IL: National Council of Teachers of English.

Brannon, L., & Pradl, G. (1984). The socialization of writing teachers. *Journal of Basic Writing, 3*(4), 28–37.

Brodkey, L. (1987a). Modernism and the scene(s) of writing. *College English, 49,* 396–418.

Brodkey, L. (1987b). Writing ethnographic narratives. *Written Communication, 9,* 25–50.

Brooke, R. (1987). "Underlife" and writing instruction. *College Composition and Communication, 38,* 141–153.

Brooke, R. (1988). Modeling a writer's identity: Reading and imitation in the writing classroom. *College Composition and Communication, 39,* 23–41.

Burnham, C. C. (1984). Recruiting, training, and supporting volunteer basic writing instructors: A working program. *Journal of Basic Writing, 3*(4), 14–27.

Calkins, L. M. (1983). *Lessons from a child.* Portsmouth, NH: Heinemann.

Chapman, D. W., & Tate, G. (1987). A survey of doctoral programs in rhetoric and composition. *Rhetoric Review, 5,* 124–186.

Corbett, E. P. J. (1987). Teaching composition: Where we've been and where we're going. *College Composition and Communication, 38,* 444–452.

Crocker, J., Fiske, S. T., & Taylor, S. E. (1984). Schematic bases of belief change. In J. R. Eiser (Ed.), *Attitudinal judgment* (pp. 197–226). New York: Springer-Verlag.

Daly, J. A., & Miller, M. D. (1975). The empirical development of an instrument to measure writing apprehension. *Research in the Teaching of English, 9,* 242–248.

Daniels, H., & Zemelman, S. (1985). *A writing project: Training teachers of composition from kindergarten to college.* Portsmouth, NH: Heinemann.

Donovan, T. R. (1984). Writing as a way of learning to teach: A program for teaching assistants. In C. H. Klaus & N. Jones (Eds.), *Courses for change in writing,* (pp. 233–240). Upper Montclair, NJ: Boynton/Cook.

Elbow, P. (1986a). Embracing contraries in the teaching process. *Embracing contraries: Explorations in learning and teaching* (pp. 142–159). New York: Oxford University Press.

Elbow, P. (1986b). Methodological doubting and believing: Contraries in inquiry. *Embracing contraries: Explorations in learning and teaching* (pp. 253–300). New York: Oxford University Press.

Emig, J. (1983). Non-magical thinking: Presenting writing developmentally in school. *The web of meaning: Essays on writing, teaching, learning, and thinking* (pp. 132–144). Montclair, NJ: Boynton/Cook.

Flower, L. (1979). Writer-based prose: A cognitive basis for problems in writing. *College English, 41,* 19–37.

Flower, L., & Hayes, J. R. (1981). A cognitive process theory of writing. *College Composition and Communication, 32,* 365–387.

Flynn, E. (1988). Composing as a woman. *College Composition and Communication, 39,* 423–435.

Fulwiler, T. (Ed.). (1987). *The journal book.* Upper Montclair, NJ: Boynton/Cook.

Fulwiler, T., Gorman, M. E., & Gorman, M. E. (1986). Changing faculty attitudes toward writing. In A. Young & T. Fulwiler (Eds.), *Writing across the disciplines: Research into practice* (pp. 53–65). Upper Montclair, NJ: Boynton/Cook.

Garnes, S. (1984). Preparing the ideal teacher of basic writing. *Journal of Basic Writing, 3*(4), 4–13.

Geertz, C. (1973). *The interpretation of cultures.* New York: Basic.

Geertz, C. (1983). *Local knowledge.* New York: Basic.

Gere, A. R., & Abbott, R. D. (1985). Talking about writing: The language of writing groups. *Research in the Teaching of English, 19,* 362–381.

Gere, A. R., Schuessler, B. F., & Abbott, R. D. (1984). Measuring teacher attitudes toward instruction in writing. In R. Beach & L. Bridwell

(Eds.), *New directions in composition research* (pp. 348–361). New York: Guilford.

Giroux, H. A. (1981). *Ideology, culture and the process of schooling.* Philadelphia: Temple University.

Goetz, J. P., & LeCompte, M. D. (1984). *Ethnography and qualitative design in educational research.* Orlando, FL: Academic.

Goffman, E. (1959). *The presentation of self in everyday life.* New York: Doubleday Anchor.

Goffman, E. (1968). *Asylum: Essays on the social situations of mental patients and other inmates.* Chicago, IL: Aldine Publishing.

Gracie, W. J., Jr. (1982). *Serving our teaching assistants and our profession: Teaching graduate students to teach composition.* Paper presented at the annual meeting of the Conference on College Composition and Communication, San Francisco, CA. (ERIC Document Reproduction Service No. ED 214 179)

Haring-Smith, T. (1985). The importance of theory in the training of teaching assistants. *ADE Bulletin, 82,* 33–39.

Harris, M. (1986). *Teaching one-to-one: The writing conference.* Urbana, IL: National Council of Teachers of English.

Harste, J., Woodward, V. A., & Burke, C. L. (1984). *Language stories and literacy lessons.* Portsmouth, NH: Heinemann.

Hartwell, P. (1985). Grammar, grammars, and the teaching of grammar. *College English, 47,* 105–127.

Heath, S. B. (1983). *Ways with words: Language, life, and work in communities and classrooms.* Cambridge, MA: Cambridge University Press.

Hillocks, G., Jr. (1986). *Research on composition: New directions for teaching.* Urbana, IL: National Council of Teachers of English.

Holland, N. (1980). Identity unity text self. In J. Tompkins (Ed.), *Reader-response criticism* (pp. 118–133). Baltimore: Johns Hopkins University Press.

Hubbuch, S. M. (1984). The anatomy of a sea change. *The Writing Instructor, 4,* 33–36.

Hunt, K. (1977). Early blooming and late blooming syntactic structures. In C. R. Cooper & L. Odell (Eds.), *Evaluating writing* (pp. 91–104). Urbana, IL: National Council of Teachers of English.

Irmscher, W. F. (1987). Finding a comfortable identity. *College Composition and Communication, 38,* 81–87.

Kamil, M., Langer, J. A., & Shanahan, T. (1985). *Understanding reading and writing research*. Boston, MA: Allyn & Bacon.

Kaufer, D. S., Hayes, J. R., & Flower, L. (1986). Composing written sentences. *Research in the Teaching of English, 20*, 121–140.

Kelly, G. (1963). *A theory of personality*. New York: Norton.

Knoblauch, C. H., & Brannon, L. (1983). Writing as learning through the curriculum. *College English, 45*, 465–474.

Knoblauch, C. H., & Brannon, L. (1984a). *Rhetorical traditions and the teaching of writing*. Upper Montclair, NJ: Boynton/Cook.

Knoblauch, C. H., & Brannon, L. (1984b). Teacher commentary on student writing: The state of the art. In D. Graves (Ed.), *Rhetoric and composition* (pp. 285–303). Upper Montclair, NJ: Boynton/Cook.

Kroll, B. M. (1980). Developmental perspectives and the teaching of composition. *College English, 41*, 741–752.

Kuhn, T. (1970). *The structure of scientific revolutions* (2nd ed.). Chicago, IL: University of Chicago Press.

Laing, R. D. (1969). *The divided self: An existential study in sanity and madness*. Middlesex, England: Penguin.

Langer, J. A., & Applebee, A. N. (1987). *How writing shapes thinking*. Urbana, IL: National Council of Teachers of English.

Larson, R. L. (1986). Making assignments, judging writing, and annotating papers: Some suggestions. In C. W. Bridges (Ed.), *Training the new teacher of College Composition* (pp. 109–116). Urbana, IL: National Council of Teachers of English.

Lindley, D. A., Jr. (1987). The source of good teaching. *English Education, 19*, 159–170.

Mayher, J. S., Lester, N., & Pradl, G. M. (1983). *Learning to write/Writing to learn*. Upper Montclair, NJ: Boynton/Cook.

McAndrew, D. A. (1987). *Visuals, questions, codes and matrices: Analyzing naturalistic data from English 101*. Unpublished manuscript, Indiana University of Pennsylvania, Department of English, Indiana, PA.

McCarthy, L. P. (1987). A stranger in strange lands: A college student writing across the curriculum. *Research in the Teaching of English, 21*, 233–265.

Mehan, H. (1982). The structure of classroom events and their consequences for student performance. In P. Gilmore and A. Glatthorn (Eds.), *Children in and out of school: Ethnography and education* (pp. 59–87). Washington, DC: Center for Applied Linguistics.

164   References

Miles, M. B., & Huberman, A. M. (1984). *Qualitative data analysis*. Beverly Hills, CA: Sage.

Moran, C. (1981). A model for teacher training programs in the field of writing. *Journal of Basic Writing, 3,* 64–78.

Munby, H. (1987). Metaphor and teachers' knowledge. *Research in the Teaching of English, 21,* 377–397.

Myers, M. (1985). *The teacher-researcher: How to study writing in the classroom.* Urbana, IL: National Council of Teachers of English.

Neel, J. P. (Ed.). (1978). *Options for the teaching of English.* New York: Modern Language Association.

Newkirk, T. (1983). Is the Bay Area model the answer? *English Education, 15,* 161–166.

North, S. M. (1987) *The making of knowledge in composition: Portrait of an emerging field.* Upper Montclair, NJ: Boynton/Cook.

Parker, R. B. (1988). Theories of writing instruction: Having them, using them, changing them. *English Education, 20,* 18–40.

Perl, S. (1979). The composing processes of unskilled college writers. *Research in the Teaching of English, 13,* 217–238.

Perl, S., & Wilson, N. (1986). *Through teachers' eyes.* Portsmouth, NH: Heinemann.

Poulin, L., & White, E. (1985). Patterns of composition instruction. *Writing Program Administration, 8,* 25–32.

Purdy, D. (1986). Opinion: A polemical history of freshman composition in our time. *College English, 48,* 791–796.

Rist, R. C. (1980). Blitzkrieg ethnography: On the transformation of a method into a movement. *Educational Researcher, 9*(2), 8–10.

Roberts, D. (1982). Survival and prosperity: TA training colloquia. *Freshman English News, 10*(3), 10–13.

Rose, M. (1980). Rigid rules, inflexible plans, and the stifling of language: A cognitivist analysis of writer's block. *College Composition and Communication, 31,* 389–401.

Russell, D. R. (1988). Review: The search for traditions. *College English, 50,* 437–443.

Ruszkiewicz, J. J. (1987). Training teachers is a process too. *College Composition and Communication, 38,* 461–464.

Schilb, J. (1988). Ideology and composition scholarship. *Journal of Advanced Composition, 8,* 22–29.

Shor, I. (1987). Educating the educators: A Frieirean approach to the crisis in teacher education. In I. Shor (Ed.), *Freire for the classroom* (pp. 7–32). Portsmouth, NH: Heinemann.

Shuy, R. W. (1981). A holistic view of learning. *Research in the Teaching of English, 15,* 101–111.

Simon, H. (1981). *The Sciences of the Artificial* (2nd ed.). Cambridge, MA: MIT Press.

Smith, W. L. (1984). Using a college writing workshop in training future English teachers. *English Education, 16,* 76–93.

Snyder, P. (1981). From fantasy to reality again: Another graduate student becomes a teacher. *Teaching English in the Two-Year College, 2,* 191–194.

Spradley, J. P. (1979). *The ethnographic interview.* New York: Holt.

Spradley, J. P. (1980). *Participant observation.* New York: Holt.

Stevens. R. (1983). *Erik Erikson: An introduction.* New York: St. Martins.

Stewig, J. W. (1981). Messages from the survivors. *English Education, 13,* 175–188.

Swanson-Owens, D. (1986). Identifying natural sources of resistance: A case study of implementing writing across the curriculum. *Research in the Teaching of English, 20,* 69–97.

Thomas, S. (1979). *Teacher interview report: Evaluation of the Bay Area Writing Project* (Technical Report). Berkeley: University of California, Berkeley, College of Education, Bay Area Writing Project. (ERIC Document Reproduction Service No. ED 191 061)

Thompson, B. M. (1979). *A theory of teacher change developed from teachers of writing.* (Research report). Urbana, IL: ERIC/RCS. (ERIC Document Reproduction Service No. ED 188 197)

Van Maanen, J. (1988). *Tales of the field: On writing ethnography.* Chicago, IL: University of Chicago.

Wilcox, K. (1982). Ethnography as a methodology and its applications to the study of schooling: A review. In G. Spindler (Ed.), *Doing the ethnography of schooling* (pp. 457–488). New York: Holt.

Williams, J. M. (1981). The Phenomenology of error. *College Composition and Communication, 32,* 152–168.

Wilson, D. (1988). *Writing projects and writing instruction: A study of teacher change.* Paper presented at the annual meeting of the Conference on College Composition and Communication, St. Louis, MO.

Wittrock, M. C. (1987). Constructing useful theories of teaching English from recent research on the cognitive processes of language. In J. R. Squire (Ed.), *The dynamics of language learning: Research in reading and English* (pp. 371–380). Urbana, IL: National Council of Teachers of English.

Wolcott, H. F. (1982). Mirrors, models, and monitors: Educator adaptations of the ethnographic innovation. In G. Spindler (Ed.), *Doing the ethnography of schooling* (pp. 69–91). New York: Holt.

Yin, R. K. (1984). *Case study research.* Beverly Hills, CA: Sage.

Young, A. (1986). Rebuilding community in the English department. In A. Young & T. Fulwiler (Eds.), *Writing across the disciplines: Research into practice* (pp. 6–20). Upper Montclair, NJ: Boynton/Cook.

Wendy Bishop is an assistant professor of English and rhetoric at Florida State University. She has published articles in *Freshman English News, Journal of Teaching Writing, Teaching English in the Two Year College,* and *The Writing Instructor,* as well as poetry and fiction in composition and creative writing journals. Her research interests include composition and creative writing pedagogy, the influence of reader-response and feminist theory on composition theory, and qualitative research and methodology.